Emerging Ministry
Being Church Today

D1304582

Nathan C. P. Frambach

Augsburg Fortress

Minneapolis

EMERGING MINISTRY
Being Church Today

Copyright © 2007 Augsburg Fortress. All rights reserved. Except for brief quotations in critical articles or reviews, no part of this book may be reproduced in any manner without prior written permission from the publisher. For more information visit: www.augsburgfortress.org/copyrights or write to: Permissions, Augsburg Fortress, Box 1209, Minneapolis, MN 55440-1209.

Large-quantity purchases or custom editions of this book are available at a discount from the publisher. For more information, contact the sales department at Augsburg Fortress, Publishers, 1-800-328-4648, or write to: Sales Director, Augsburg Fortress, Box 1209, Minneapolis, MN 55440-1209.

Scripture quotations, unless otherwise marked, are from the New Revised Standard Version Bible, copyright © 1989 by the Division of Christian Education of the National Council of the Churches of Christ in the U.S.A. Used by permission. All rights reserved.

Library of Congress Cataloging-in-Publication Data
Frambach, Nathan C. P., 1964-
  Emerging ministry : being church today / Nathan C.P. Frambach.
     p. cm. — (Lutheran voices)
  Includes bibliographical references.
  ISBN 978-0-8066-8004-0 (pbk. : alk. paper)
  1. Mission of the church. I. Title.
  BV601.8.F73 2007
  250—dc22   2007005521

Cover Design: © Koechel Peterson and Associates, Inc., Minneapolis, MN
              www.koechelpeterson.com
Cover photo: © age fotostock/SuperStock

The paper used in this publication meets the minimum requirements of American National Standard for Information Sciences—Permanence of Paper for Printed Library Materials, ANSI Z329.48-1984.

Manufactured in the U.S.A.

11   10   09   08   3   4   5   6   7   8   9   10

Vocatus Atque Non Vocatus Deus Aderit
"Bidden or not bidden, God is present."

Dedicated to

For Pastor Karen Ward and countless other Christ followers
who are paving the road to a 21st Century Church.

Contents

Preface

You are so young, so before all beginning, and I want to beg you, as much as I can . . . to be patient toward all that is unsolved in your heart and to try to love the questions themselves like locked rooms and like books that are written in a very foreign tongue. Do not now seek the answers, which cannot be given you because you would not be able to live them. And the point is, to live everything. Live the questions now. Perhaps you will then gradually, without noticing it, live along some distant day into the answer.[1]

I live with my fair share of questions, many of which, indeed, go unanswered. As a rule I'm okay with this—I appreciate questions and would rather have a good question go unanswered than be given a pat answer to a complicated question any day of the week. But, honestly, I can only live with questions for so long before we need to tussle. The main reason I am writing this book—which I see as a way to join in a conversation with a lot of people, including you—is because of some questions about God's mission in the world, the ministry of the churches, and Christian leadership that won't let go of me. They have been percolating, and the time has come to fuss with them.

What I write in the pages that follow is one way of heeding the poet's advice, living the questions by pondering them and writing about them and inviting others—inviting you—into a conversation that hopefully they will generate. Obviously this will not be a let's-get-together-over-a-cup-of-coffee-and-talk kind of conversation. That would be nice—those are the kinds of chats that I most enjoy—but it won't be a kitchen-table or church-basement kind of conversation. Rather, my hope and prayer is that what I write here will instigate a whole bunch of conversations among creative, passionate, missional Christian leaders in all different kinds of neighborhoods and Christian communities. In short, I hope to spark some imagination and prompt conversation among people like you—Christ followers, the people of God—on mission, God-spotting, picking up the trail of the Holy Spirit and helping pave the road to the church that God intends. And perhaps gradually, each in our own places, but all together, without even noticing it, we will live into God's promised future.

After an introductory chapter on the current landscape in which we seek to live God's mission today, we're going to explore what the church is (missional, public, evangelical) as well as what the church is not (private, family) called to be in chapter 2. After that we will consider how to go about being church today by focusing on story and listening. In chapter 4, we'll see what we can learn from emerging church communities about what it means to be the church today as Christian communities. And in the last chapter we will take a look at emerging ministry and leadership as we seek to navigate the new wilderness roads along which God's Spirit is leading us today.

Finally, if you would like to join in an online discussion of the ideas set forth in this book, please note that a Web site devoted to it has been set up by the publisher. Go to www.emergingministryonline.org.

Acknowledgments

A former colleague once said, "The end of thinking is thanking," and the time has come to express my gratitude. At Wartburg Theological Seminary we are seeking to live into God's promised future as we form valued leaders for God's mission. I'm indebted to our Board of Directors, President Duane Larson, Dean Craig Nessan, and my faculty colleagues for a sabbatical, during which time I was able to complete this manuscript. Year after year the students at Wartburg have indulged my enduring curiosity about the emerging church conversation, and gently but consistently they have pushed me to see it within the larger context of the emerging missional ecclesiology about which I write in this book. Beyond my life at Wartburg there is a small group of friends—Karen Ward, Ryan Torma, Todd Zielinski, Pam Fickenscher, Thomas Knoll, and probably a few others—who have been instigating the emerging leaders network these past few years and with whom I have shared conversation and journey that has sparked my imagination and stirred my soul.

This season of sabbatical has added a different rhythm to my life—slower and a bit more offbeat and relaxed—though inspiring and generative. By day I have spent much time at New Melleray Abbey, a Cistercian (Trappist) monastery located in the rolling farmland south of Dubuque, Iowa. I'm obliged to the monks of New Melleray for their hospitality, for space to read and write, for the opportunity to pray the hours and allow things to rest before God. Most evenings and weekends have been spent with my family, for whose presence in my life I am grateful. My youngest son, Andres, told me recently that he wished he could write a book someday, which I took to be a kind of compliment. I wish that for him, too. I spent a few hours one morning at Miguel's coffee shop with my oldest son, Garrett, so he could "interview" me about the writing of this book for Ms. DeKeyser's fifth grade class at John F. Kennedy elementary school. It very well might be my only interview, and if that is the case, it will be sufficient. It is my beloved wife, Diane, with whom I share this journey most deeply and profoundly. She has given up her late afternoon read-the-paper-and-catch-a-short-nap-before-the-school-bus-pulls-up time and resisted the temptation of being too envious of my being on sabbatical. Both of these are small expressions of the grace by which she lives each day.

And the end of thanking is . . . ? Writing. Buckle up, friends, it's time to go.

1

Living God's Mission Today:
An Emerging Landscape

An Opening Parable

He came back, this time with his mom. I finally learned his name—Matt—although his mother called him Matty. Just a bit over five years ago, four ruffians sauntered across a rather large expanse of open field parallel to the railroad tracks and parallel to the creek beside the Pulpit Rock apartments at Wartburg Seminary in Dubuque, Iowa. I first noticed them out of the corner of my eye as they broke out of the woods into the clearing and slowly, methodically wandered our way and into my life. They asked for a drink of water and we ended up sitting on the floor of our Pulpit Rock apartment, drinking soda and looking out the window up toward the Wartburg Seminary castle. We decided that it wouldn't be a good idea to try and climb the tower, and they wondered what exactly a seminary was and what went on in such a place, anyway. I told them in my own feeble way how we sought, as a seminary community, to listen to God and to one another, to love God and one another, to follow God and serve others, and perhaps in the process to learn something of God's ways and God's desire. And if we couldn't do those things too well then we went to our classes and our meetings, ate our lunch together and drank our coffee, wrote our papers and prayed our prayers and sang our songs in worship and went home at the end of the day hopefully no worse for the wear. We trusted, so often without ever saying it, that somehow, in the midst of this life together, God was altogether present, even if we were not, moving in our midst, touching our lives in surprising and unexpected ways, calling us out, sending us out, calling us out.

I remember how one of them rolled his eyes really big and sighed really deep, and when I called him on it, he said that his dad told him that when someone started talking about God in a conversation it was time to go (with the thumb saying "outta here"). Then the ringleader—Matty—called his friend on his eye-rolling, deep-sighing attitude and said that as far as he knew he didn't have a dad and he wanted to hear what I had to say about God. And because they sort of voted (three to one, I abstained), I hauled out a bunch of Bibles and we sat there on the floor and looked at Bible stories and talked about God for a bit. There was nothing more dramatic about it. Pretty soon it was obviously time to be done, and as they left, Matty noticed a picture my oldest son Garrett and me. In the picture Garrett, two-years-old, is sitting on my lap. He is leaning up to tell me something and I am tilting my head down to listen to him. It appears as though our cheeks are touching.

Matty looked at me and asked, "So, are you a dad?"

"Yeah," I responded, "I'm a dad."

"I bet you're a pretty good one," he remarked, somewhat matter-of-factly, and then he left. Whether or not I'm a good dad will be up to God and history and my children. I certainly figured I would never see Matty again.

But I did. He and his mother showed up on our doorstep out in Asbury, Iowa, on a Saturday morning early in the summer, nearly a year after he had first wandered into my life. He had taken one of my Bibles with him that first day we met, and I guess it had my name in it. She apologized profusely and said that Matty would not rest until they had found me, and, truth be told, she wanted to see the picture, the one that, in her words, had turned their lives upside down in a good sort of way. After that first meeting, Matty had returned home bent on two things: connecting with God and finding his father.

They'd reconnected with their Roman Catholic roots and were happily a part of a faith community. But after almost a year of trying, she could not find the father of her son. They had been seeing a counselor, who suggested that perhaps it was time to stop trying so hard and find another way to bring about some closure. This was fine with Matty—but he needed to find me.

And so it was that almost a year later they ended up on my doorstep out in Asbury, on a clear, early summer Saturday morning. Matty wanted to see the picture again. I brought it out, along with Garrett in person. Matty smiled when he saw it. He reached into his backpack and pulled out a camera. His mother was taken aback, "I didn't know he brought that camera," she said.

"You touched my life," Matty said to me, "but I never got to touch you." I held out my hand. Remembering the earlier picture, Matty proffered his cheek. I knelt down and we had our picture made, sticky, Saturday-morning cheek to sticky, unshaven, Saturday-morning cheek. For Matty, it seemed, it was a simple, safe touch that closed the deal.

This experience has become a parable for me as I think about ministry today, particularly with people in the emerging cultures all around us. It has become parable in the way that John Dominic Crossan understands parable:

Parables—give God room. They are stories, which shatter the deep structures of our accepted world and thereby render clear and evident to us the relativity of story itself. They remove our defenses and make us vulnerable to God. It is only in such experiences that God can touch us, and only in such moments does the Kingdom of God arrive.[1]

The church today needs both parabolic speech and parabolic action that shatters our complacency and conventionality, rendering clear and bringing near the power of God's story and the promise of God's reign.

Frontier Living Old and New

Wilhelm Loehe, founder of the institution at which I am called to teach, was oft to say, "Mission is nothing but the one church of God in motion,"[2] a phrase that in capsule reflected a missional ecclesiology (an understanding of what it means to be the church that is rooted in God's mission in the world and focused on the reign of God) that served Loehe and his missionally-minded cohorts well in their particular frontier context (the United States in the mid-1800s). Now, in this new, emerging frontier context in which the churches of North America find themselves, a missional ecclesiology must emerge in practice that is more deeply Trinitarian and eschatological, more organic and fluid as it lives. In short, a way of being church must emerge that orients the *whole life* of a Christian community around God's mission. The question that will drive such an emergence is, "What does it mean to be the church as we live?"—not as we think or remember or long for, but as we live as the people of God. Mission in this new frontier context is the way a people sent by a sending God live everyday, on mission, as they risk living for the reign of God and bear witness to the gospel of Jesus Christ "24/7" as many are apt to say. What God has done in Jesus Christ for the sake of creation and all of its peoples cannot be undone; it is *pro nobis,* for you, for me, for all. It is this central proclamation of the Christian faith to which the Holy Spirit continually points us, and in turn, to which we are called continually to point others. What matters first and perhaps most is who we are: a people created, chosen, cleansed, claimed, and called by God in Christ. And we are who we are, for better or for worse, all the time, not just on Sunday mornings or Wednesday evenings. On the new wilderness roads emerging everywhere all around us, being "on mission" looks, I believe, strikingly similar to what happened on that much older wilderness road in the Acts of the Apostles (8:26ff). Someone is sent, and goes, to an unexpected place along the Way, and is encountered in a deeply mutual and relational way by another in whose midst the Spirit works mutual transformation.

I want to suggest that we have at least two fundamental foci in our DNA as Lutheran Christians in this country, a people sent to and always living in particular places that are historically conditioned. First, there is this strong missionary impulse to bear witness to the Christian gospel "Lutheranly," remaining faithful to the primary accents of our Lutheran heritage: the doctrine of justification by grace through faith, a deep commitment to the efficacy of the word of God as both law and promise, an understanding of the human as *simul justus et peccatur* (at the same time justified and sinful), a profound sensibility about the priesthood of all believers, and a clear understanding of *vocatio* (calling) as the primary means of the ministry of the baptized. This missional impulse is coupled with a built-in sensibility about learning to navigate the realities of frontier living. It's one of the mantras we recite (and believe) at Wartburg Seminary: attending to context. Many of our Lutheran forebears knew well how to migrate their faith into a new place. They became bilingual, both literally and figuratively, learning a new language as well as the customs and mores of new people. They learned not only how to survive in but how to adapt to a new environment; yet they held onto those threads indispensable to their beliefs and way of life. Perhaps many of our forebears were culturally savvy before adapting to a new place was considered savvy. Regardless, we must affirm, celebrate, and build on these dual commitments: the strong missional impulse and the knack for navigating new frontiers. However, we must also fess up to another reality: the landscape has changed.

An Emerging Landscape

The phrase "paradigm shift," although overused, seems an accurate description for the acute changes experienced by Christian churches attempting to navigate the twentieth century. Underlying these changes was a massive shifting of the tectonic plates, culturally speaking, what theologian Graham Ward calls a "cultural sea change."[3] This should come as no surprise; the church had a place, had its place in Christendom, and then lost this place. For a period of time ranging roughly from the mid-fourth century to mid-twentieth century, often referred to as the age of Christendom, Christianity and the Christian church as an institution had a culturally supported, central place in the public life of many Western societies. In the United States there existed an accommodating, intimate relationship between the church and the predominant culture of the larger society. As a result, this relationship led to an environment in which these two entities, church and culture, were functionally one and the same. Today, however, we simply cannot talk about culture without using the plural, "cultures." We live within what some have called a "pluriverse" of cultures determined by geography, race, ethnicity, class, worldview, and the like. All of us inhabit and are shaped by a variety of cultures at the same time. Given the impact of some large, powerful realities—secularization, cultural and religious pluralism, the massive advances in technology that created the digitally-enhanced world we now experience in this "Infomedia" age—the church (and here I refer to the Christian churches) has been de-centered. Under increasing pressure from these aforementioned powerful realities, the cultural underpinnings that once supported it swept away, the church practiced some ecclesiastical free agency and swapped its central place in public life for a prominent place in the private domain of life.

More broadly, there was another phenomenon defining an emerging missiological landscape. As early as 1942, William Temple, then Archbishop of Canterbury, pointed to the emergence of worldwide Christianity and named it the "great new fact of our time."[4] The "fact" to which he was referring was but an incipient reality at the time: Christianity had been transformed. No longer confined to the Northern Atlantic context, it had become a global mélange of churches, existing in virtually every major cultural reality on earth. Every year David Barrett generates a statistical review for the International Bulletin of Missionary Research. How's this for an eye-opener: In 1900, Christians in Europe/North America comprised 77 percent of the world Christian population. By sometime in 1998, Christians in Europe/North America comprised 38 percent of the world Christian population. By the year 2025, it is projected that Christians in Europe/North America will comprise 27 percent of the world Christian population.[5]

More recently, Philip Jenkins has narrated this transformation that is taking place in world Christianity.[6] Notice that churches in non-Atlantic regions (Africa, India, South America, etc.) are growing, often exponentially in some cases, while many or even most established Christian traditions are losing numbers, especially in recent decades. At the same time, these established Christian traditions are coming to terms with the awareness that Christendom—the dominance of Christian religion and institutional churches in the West—is finally over. To this end, Douglas John Hall's trilogy, *Thinking/Professing/Confessing the Faith*, documents this with painstaking detail.

These changes are difficult to grasp, and maybe even harder to digest for many of us—particularly members and leaders of the so-called mainline churches in North America. Tribes like the Lutherans, Presbyterians, Methodists, and Episcopalians specifically enjoyed the benefits of establishment and protection under the cover of Christendom. For these churches, the paradigm shift we have been discussing is extremely challenging. Navigating this emerging missiological landscape will involve discerning and experimenting with approaches to ministry that will radically challenge many present understandings of what it means to be the church today. Navigating this landscape will mean:

- Learning how to do theology in unaccustomed ways. This will expose different sources for theological reflection, including creative sources that focus on the search for God in popular culture. Graham Ward suggests that this will involve both a return to and a new emphasis on re-enchantment with filmmakers, novelists, poets, philosophers, political theorists, and cultural analysts—not necessarily theologians—leading the way.

- Discovering how to relate to a context genuinely and deeply, such as we see in Acts 17 (Paul at the Areopagus). We relate to this context—previously Christian and then secularized Western cultures—as marginalized outsiders (e.g., church decentered), which means we begin with a primary leadership posture characterized by humility, patience, and servanthood.

- Learning and practicing new forms of communication, beginning with deep listening and mutual dialog as the first move toward genuine understanding. This exposes the need for the communication of the Christian message to be intelligible, at the heart of which very well might be the recovery of gospel as story or narrative into which the hearer is invited to dwell.

- Discerning and asking hard, honest questions about the purpose of the church from the perspective of particular traditions and then thinking and acting differently in terms of how to go about fulfilling said purpose, once discerned.

The fact of the matter is, if we are to be true to our historical legacy as Lutheran Christians in this country—a people possessing a strong missional impulse coupled with a knack for navigating new frontiers—then we must wrestle with this missional paradigm shift. Why? Because it defines the North American religious context in which we are called to live God's mission today. The challenge before us is, at its core, a missiological challenge. There has emerged around us a substantial, global conversation about the mission of the church, at the heart of which is a shift *from* a primary focus on the church and its expansion *to* a focus on God as a missionary God.

Such a shift in focus to God as a missionary God has tremendous implications for the life and ministry of Christian communities and their leadership. If God is a missionary God, then the church is called to be a missionary church and Christian leaders are called to exercise missionary leadership. This way of thinking about and imagining Christian life and practice has come to be called the theology of the *missio Dei*, or the sending of God. In its infancy, this theology was significantly influenced by Karl Barth in the West. More recently, the work of David Bosch has been the most influential, with his 1991 book, *Transforming Mission: Paradigm Shifts in Theology of Mission*, already a classic.

> Mission was understood as being derived from the very nature of God. It was thus put in the context of the doctrine of the Trinity, not of ecclesiology or soteriology. The classical doctrine of the *missio Dei* as God the Father sending the Son, and God the Son sending the Spirit was expanded to include yet another "movement": Father, Son, and Holy Spirit sending the church into the world.[7]

In short, no Trinity, no mission; no Trinity, no church. The movement to mission is rooted in the very life of the triune God. God knows relationship within God's self, that is, "immanently." Yet this deeply relational God is one who lives by sharing. As Justo Gonzalez so nicely puts it, for too long "Christians have made the basic mistake of approaching the Trinity as a puzzle to be solved rather than as an example to be imitated. . . . If the Trinity is the doctrine of a God whose very life is a life of sharing, its clear consequence is that those who claim belief in such a God must live a similar life."[8]

God, in creating, seeks relationship beyond God's self, that is, "economically." Out of God flows love, into the creation and all of its peoples.[9] In particular, the people of God are called in love to share this love. Can you see where this gets us? The purpose of mission and evangelical living is not merely for the sake of the church. Rather, it is to express God's faithfulness to God's saving intention for the entire creation.

The landscape has changed, due in no small part to those powerful realties about which we spoke earlier. In so many ways it's a big world getting smaller and coming closer all of the time. We now have at least one generation in this country, if not two, that has been bathed in bytes since birth. A new frontier context has emerged, and we are once again immigrants, in a way, in a world that we do not always understand. And we live in the midst of so many people who are, literally, immigrants, just like our ancestors once were.

In this new frontier context there are new wilderness roads along which we are sent to bear witness to the reign of God that broke into the world in and through the person of Jesus Christ. It is this reality, the inbreaking of the reign of God, that the gospel announces. We are called and sent to proclaim this good news, the same message Jesus carried with him: "The kingdom of God has come near" (cf. Matt. 4:17; Mark 1:14-15; Luke 10:1-12). Sinners are forgiven, and enemies too for that matter; the last are first; the least are greatest. There are people to be loved, and words of healing and hope to be spoken. What does the reign of God look like? It looks like the Sermon on the Mount (Matt. 5–7), and perhaps specifically the Beatitudes (Matt. 5:3-12), as well as the vivid picture captured in Revelation 21:1-7.

But the landscape is not the only thing that has changed. A profound shift has taken place in how one understands mission. The modern missionary movement that spawned our being Lutherans in this country today focused primarily on the church and its expansion. In our emerging missiological landscape we are compelled to focus on God as a missionary God and the church as that community sent by God the sending One to embody a more fluid witness in new frontier contexts—on mission wherever, whenever. In other words, the church does not do mission, it is mission; by its very nature and calling it lives as God's sent people. Worship centered in Word and Sacrament, life as a distinctive community, the concrete demonstration of God's love in acts of service—all bear witness to the good news of God in Jesus Christ. The church is sign and foretaste of this good news, at the heart of which is the inbreaking of the reign of God. The church is called to witness to, participate in, even celebrate God's mission, all the while knowing that the "mission" does not belong to the church, but to God.

God intends Christianity to be more than a system of belief or even a way of life. Rather, Christian beliefs and practices are intended to foster a way of being human that sends us into the world to imitate the deep relationality of God—a God who is for the world and for other people. It is the already-but-not-yet reign of God to which we point and to which we are called to bear witness. This missional focus on the reign of God suggests that the church is never to be the withdrawn or isolated end-user of the Christian gospel. Rather, we hear and receive by faith the good news of the gospel so that we may be equipped and sent into the world to love our neighbors, serve the other, and care for the whole creation. The church doesn't have a mission; the church is mission, and thus both object and agent of God's mission.

Missionary Living in a New Frontier Context

Back to a question I posed at the beginning of this chapter: What does it mean to be the church as we live? Where are the new wilderness roads that are emerging around us? Where are the new wilderness roads to which you are being called, along which perhaps you are already walking? They are everywhere and all around us. Generating a response to these and so many other questions means not thinking more, but *thinking and acting differently*. In this new frontier context the people of God must be much more fluid, more nimble, more agile than we have heretofore. We must reach back, farther back than our immigrant or even Reformation past, to find cues and clues for navigating the new wilderness roads in this emerging frontier context. The book of Acts is a good place to start. I mean here the book of Acts not as a road map to help us with our navigating, and certainly not as a prescription for being church today. Rather, it seems to me that we will discover, or rediscover in the biblical narrative some cues and clues for missionary living in this new frontier context emerging a thousand different ways all around us. As a kind of case study in miniature, I point to Acts 8:26-40—the story of Phillip and the Ethiopian Eunuch.

Questions for Reflection & Discussion

1. The story of Philip and the Ethiopian Eunuch (Acts 8:26-40) is a key text when it comes to figuring out what it means to live God's mission today, and a text to which we shall return at the end of this book. Take some time to read the text carefully, and then discuss it. What cues and clues do you see and hear for living God's mission today?

2. What is the "mission history" of your church community? Discuss the manner in which your congregation came into being—when, where, who, how, and why?

3. When was the last time you had an experience or an encounter like the one described in the opening parable (see pp. 13-15)? How have you come to interpret or understand what happened?

4. What does it mean to be the church as we live? Where are the new wilderness roads that are emerging around us? Where are the new wilderness roads to which you are being called, along which perhaps you are already walking?

2

Being Church Today: The Gathered and Gathering Community

A Common, but Troublesome, Metaphor

What does it mean to be the church today? That is a heart-and-soul question for me, and is quickly accompanied by a host of other questions: What is "the church" to which reference is so often and easily made? What it is about? What it is for? One of the most familiar metaphors for church, and one I used earlier in my life, is that of the church as family. On one level I'm quite comfortable with this metaphor. To my mind, family of God language and metaphor as in "Whoever does the will of my Father in heaven is my brother and sister and mother" (Matt. 12:50; cf. Luke 8:19-21; Mark 3:31-34) opens and increases our imagination about what it means to be the church—akin to body of Christ, communion of saints, and people of God. But I have become uncomfortable with equating the local church, a particular congregation or community, with a smaller, more modern notion of family because I believe that applying the metaphor in this manner potentially diminishes our imagination about what it means to be the church.

Historically speaking, congregations are relatively new on the religious landscape, as is the notion of "family," at least the way it has been popularly understood and sought in America. In the past few decades there has arisen a renewed and helpful emphasis on the significance of the congregation.[1] Unfortunately, the understanding that a congregation should be like a family to its members has become commonplace. Is this a helpful way to understand congregations?

The use of the family metaphor for describing religious communities has come to us in large part from the work of family systems thinkers and therapists, including the late Edwin Friedman whose book, *Generation to Generation,* has been a popular and, in many respects, helpful book to many pastoral leaders. In *Generation to Generation,* Friedman applied concepts of systemic family therapy to the emotional life of congregations and their leaders in order to develop a family systems perspective of organized religious life. As a student of Murray Bowen and Bowenian thinking, Friedman draws heavily on theory that was developed and practiced in a psychological rather than a theological setting. Hence, Friedman's work is built on and employs constructs that originated within a therapeutic paradigm. And therein, I believe, lies the crux of the problem.

While I acknowledge that there are ideas or insights that can be translated from family systems theory to understanding emotional processes in congregational life, I think the greater contribution of Friedman's work and others is that it helps shift the focus of ministry in religious congregations from the parts to the whole. That shift in focus offers a needed corrective to the rampant and dominant individualism[2] so pervasive in this American religious context. However, as alluded to earlier, Friedman refers to churches, synagogues, rectories, and hierarchies *as* families.[3] While he intends by this to indicate that a religious congregation (in terms of emotional processes) can function like a family, the nuance is too often missed. What remains is sentiment akin to that which I recently saw quoted in the religion section of my local newspaper, "My congregation is like my family. Everyone is so close."

I am amazed at how prevalent it has become to refer to a congregation as "our church family." We have allowed this metaphor of family to sneak in and settle into the way we understand what it means to be the church. As a case in point, consider the congregation where I served for four years during my doctoral work. This suburban, mostly affluent, and growing exponentially congregation worshiped more than twenty-two hundred people each week at six different service times. In other words, there were essentially six different congregations. During my time there, new member classes were received virtually every month, with seldom fewer than twelve to fifteen people in attendance and often as many as thirty or forty. And yet, each time people were ritually welcomed during a service of worship, the congregation was asked to find these persons after worship and "welcome them to our church family." It is reflexive, an unconscious, albeit uncritical practice. Consider as an additional example the first congregation where I served as a pastor. It was a rural, tight-knit, highly agricultural community that pretty much stayed the same from year to year. There were typically as many people at the weekly staff meeting of that large suburban congregation as there were at Easter worship in the small rural church I served. During my tenure there we received only a few families into church membership, and yet I can recall with relative accuracy that they were somehow welcomed into "our church family." In both instances this powerful metaphor from another paradigm had seeped into the thinking and practice of religious congregations and implanted itself.

What is the sense of this family metaphor in such very different faith communities? Of what value is such an understanding of church? More importantly, what misconceptions does it create for congregational members, especially in large congregations, who are largely unknown to one another, or even recognized by one another?

If one understands the congregation as a private, family chapel—which unfortunately seems to be the case for many in our contemporary setting—then perhaps the family metaphor is a helpful one.

I am suggesting here that that is not the case; the family metaphor is not helpful and it is theologically inadequate to boot. One of the most influential religious thinkers of the twentieth century, Wolfhart Pannenberg, provides a theological basis for understanding that church communities are called to be just the opposite of a private, family chapel. They are, in fact, called to be a public outpost for mission. For Pannenberg, the true identity of the human person is exocentric, that is, located and grounded outside of one's self. He attributes the discovery of this notion as it relates to the religious dimension of human life to Luther.

> . . . when Luther described the existence of believers by saying that they exist in faith *extra se in Christo* ("outside themselves in Christ"). This is precisely a description of the essential structure of faith as trust; for whenever we trust, we "abandon ourselves" and build on the person or thing in which we trust. Through our trust we make our existence dependent on that to which we abandon ourselves.[4]

But opposed to this exocentric identity, there is inside the human person an egocentric yearning to be turned in on the self (based on another insight into the human condition used by Luther and other Reformation thinkers, *homo incurvatus in se,* "the human turned in on the self"). In short, this is a way of understanding how sin operates in human beings.

To be open to the other, to the world, and ultimately to God is human destiny, the image of God to which we are called. Because we are created in the image of God, our destiny is communal; we are created for life together. Pannenberg's understanding of the individual human applies also to human systems—for our purposes here, church communities. Churches, too, are called to be open to the other, to the world around them, and ultimately to God. Church communities also live within the egocentric/exocentric tension. The family metaphor is an appealing siren song that can lull a congregation into valuing privacy and intimacy above all else. When this happens, it is tempting for us church people to turn in on ourselves and become a private enclave, rather than a public meeting place where there is great passion and compassion for the outsider, the stranger, the marginalized, and the newcomer.

Congregations that desire chiefly to be like a family can all too easily value privacy and intimacy above all else. This makes life easy for the insider who knows the code language (e.g., *LBW* and *WOV* and now *ELW*) and the particular quirks of church life (when to stand and sit, who sits in which pew), but it makes life very difficult and uncomfortable for the outsider, the stranger, the newcomer. This family mentality has a sneaky way of undermining—often without anyone intending or even realizing it—a congregation's larger sense of hospitality, public witness, and vision of service to the world.

So the frequent and often uncritical use of the family metaphor for religious communities makes me nervous. It focuses too much on personal, individual piety and tends to make a Christian community more like a privileged club or a clandestine organization. About the last thing we need right now is to make Christianity more of a family affair between "me and Jesus." I'm not the only one who is nervous about this; Herbert Anderson has addressed this issue as well:

> He [Freidman] is right to identify the emotional interlocking of the clergy's family, the families in the congregation and the congregational "family." All three are human systems and all three share characteristics common to human systems. My uneasiness with his use of the family metaphor for the religious community is . . . based on . . . the consequences for the congregation's vision of service to the world if it thinks about itself primarily as "family." It is difficult enough to inspire congregations to look beyond their own boundaries to wider and wider communities of human need. . . . By using the family metaphor . . . there is the danger of diluting the lively

tension between the family as a necessary human community for the sake of criticism and care and the kingdom of God that calls us to respond to ever widening circles of human concern.[5]

In the final analysis, it is the missionary power of the Christian message and the evangelical, public orientation of church communities that is undermined by the family metaphor. In other words, the use of the family metaphor for church communities is detrimental to the public mission of the Christian gospel.

That said, it would be remiss of me not to acknowledge that there are some very understandable reasons why so many of us are drawn to the family metaphor, why we want our congregations to be like a big, happy family. Some of us literally don't have much in terms of a family or a home. For others, what is there isn't very pleasant or healthy. I'm guessing that for most of us our experience of family is ambiguous at best—sometimes joyous, other times painful, most of the time hard work. It is tempting and very natural to have an idealized notion of what family should be—a place with no conflict and very little change, where you are known and accepted, peculiar habits and obvious blemishes included. If we don't experience the ideal that we seek in our homes, then quite naturally we look for it somewhere else. What better place than our church?

The human reality is that people do have a deep desire and need for a place where one truly belongs—a safe place where one experiences genuine care and acceptance. I want to suggest that church communities can offer this sense of belonging and acceptance without needing to be like a family. From the perspective of the Christian faith, genuine care and profound acceptance are rooted not in any notion or particular configuration of family but in the gospel of Jesus Christ. What makes a church community unique is that it is focused on and centered in God's gospel. It is first God the Spirit who calls, gathers, enlightens, and makes holy each congregation as well as the whole Christian church on earth. Christian communities are called to offer this to all people because it is the essence of the gospel's invitation and proclamation. And I believe that the mission if the Christian gospel is best served when churches understand themselves as community rather than family.

An Alternative Understanding

Quite frankly, I'm not convinced it is either best or very wise to want our church communities to be like families. Rather, I want families—whatever their form or state of health—to be like families. Churches then are freed to do all that they can to support and strengthen families, whatever their configuration, so that caring ministry and effective faith formation can happen in the home. Because the partnership between a religious community and the home is so critical, church communities can then focus their energy on encouraging, supporting, and training the home for faith formation. In particular, time and energy needs to be focused on inspiring, equipping, and training parents and other primary life caregivers to model and teach the faith to all of God's kids. In this way, the Christian home is church, too. It is, to use the helpful image of Marjorie Thompson, the *domestic church*. This understanding of the Christian home as domestic church has a rich biblical legacy in the notion of "house churches." In the early, New Testament church, the home was the center of Christian life and faith formation. When the home is understood as the domestic church, congregations are freed to become the *"communal church,"* the public gatherings where all people—especially the stranger—are welcomed and embraced by God through the proclamation of the gospel.

It is my contention that God intends for a Christian community to be more, to be bigger than a family. Congregations are public outposts for mission. The church as *ecclesia* is the gathered community. Perhaps this is the metaphor that I like better than family—the church as gathered and gathering community. It's not as neat and tidy nor catchy as church family, but I daresay it is more adequate theologically, and more descriptive of what God does in and through the people of God. As Paul Hanson demonstrated so nicely in his book, *The People Called*,[6] the biblical notion of community seems more accurate and more richly descriptive in depicting what it means to be church than any modern notion of family. On the one hand, the people of God gather as communities of faith. Particular bands and households from the people of God come together in public places to worship, learn, serve, play, and pray. On the other hand, the people of God as communities of faith are called to gather—to reach out and extend to one and all that simple, public message that is at the heart of God's gospel: "Come and see; come and follow; go and tell and live the good news."

If the gospel is the essential core of the church and the local congregation central to the life of the church, I am suggesting that the church (congregation) is necessarily public in its nature because the gospel is inherently public in its nature. I believe that God intends for the people of God—for all Christian communities—to be public, missional, and evangelical rather than private and familial.

Living the Mission

Churches are communities of human beings that exist in relationship to a larger community around them. They live in the tension about which I spoke earlier, the tension between being turned in and called and sent out. My imagination and vision for religious congregations is that they are open, welcoming, public places, decidedly evangelical in the best sense of the word, with the triune God at the center. The openness to which congregations are called is directed not only to the stranger, the outsider, the seeker, but perhaps more importantly to God, who is, in fact, the "main thing." They know and believe deeply that God has filled their storehouse with the missionary power of the Christian message, and they live and act out of this abundance. It is the living voice of the gospel, the voice of Jesus, to which we must listen most closely, and this voice continually calls us out of our comfort zones and private enclaves and into public service and engagement with others in God's world.

So how do we do this? What does it mean to be a public outpost for mission? What does it mean to be the church today? I believe that it is less about being tied to a place and more about participating in a way of life. It means an understanding of "the church" that is more nimble, more agile, perhaps even more mobile, yet deeply rooted in God's Word of promise in Jesus Christ. If we are the gathered and gathering community as the people of God, then we need to learn better how to go *out the out door*—living God's mission wherever, whenever. We need to learn how to be a place yet leave our church buildings and live God's mission. We are called to be good news in God's world. We gather as God's people, we listen to God's story, we leave because we are sent to "become what we receive," the body of Christ, listening to others, loving our neighbors, living God's story.

Questions for Reflection & Discussion

1. What is your favorite metaphor—biblical or otherwise—for the church? What image or metaphor do you think best describes the church community to which you belong right now?

2. What do you make of the author's critique of using the family metaphor for a local church community? Do you agree or disagree? Is there value for such an understanding that the author misses? Or do you see additional concerns and potential problems that the author fails to point out?

3. How can congregations see to it that caring ministry and faith formation is happening in the home? How can church communities inspire, encourage, support, equip, and train parents and other primary life caregivers to model and teach the faith to the younger

generations? How is this currently happening in your church community?

4. Do you consider your congregation a "gathered and gathering community?" Is your church community a "public outpost for mission?" How do you gather? How are you a public presence and/or witness for Jesus Christ? How are you in mission with God in your community and neighborhood?

3

God-Spotting: Evangelical Listening and Storied Living

We are living in an era of unprecedented change. The global village of which we are a part, the North American context in which we live, the Christian church in which we participate—all are reeling from the constant onslaught of change and transition. We are living in an "in-between" time as human history moves from one age to another: from the industrial age to the infomedia age; from the modern world to the hyper-modern to the post-whateverism world. Futurist Alvin Toffler calls the period from 1950 to roughly 2025 a "hinge of history" as an old world is dying and a new world is being born.

Granted, not all peoples in all places experience these shifts in the same way. Like it or not, certain nations and cultures are privileged over others, often the result of wielding more forcefully their power and peddling their influence to others. Nonetheless, such unprecedented change affects virtually everyone, and most everyone wants and needs to learn how to navigate a landscape that is constantly shifting. In such a fluid situation, the human tendency is to create "in" groups and "out" groups: circle the wagons, draw the boundaries, and clearly define the rules. Unfortunately, rules will not help us navigate this new landscape. In the midst of tumultuous transition, I believe that we need *more stories,* not more rules.

Jesus told the crowds all these things in parables; without a parable he told them nothing. This was to fulfill what had been spoken through the prophet: "I will open my mouth to speak in parables; I will proclaim what has been hidden from the foundation of the world" (Matt. 13:34-35).

Jesus knew the power of story. His teaching reflected his embodiment of the unexpected presence of God's grace. I believe that the church today needs both parabolic speech and parabolic action—powerful stories that shatter our complacency and conventionality, rendering clear and bringing new the power of God's story and the promise of God's reign.

Human Beings Are Storied Creatures

I teach at a seminary, and the telling and hearing of stories happens aplenty here. But I suspect that the same is true for you in your situation because human beings, by our very nature, are storied creatures. People everywhere tell stories. People of all ages listen to stories. Individuals, families, and nations all have stories that are passed on from one generation to the next. In essence, each of us has a history that can be seen from one perspective as a bricolage of stories.

As human beings we make meanings of our experiences by constructing and living narratives or stories. These stories are like tapes that we play back quite naturally, sometimes unconsciously, throughout our lives. Not only do we story our lives, but we also live within these stories, "performing" them. In other words, our stories inform what we do, and what we do informs our stories. Our knowledge of the world, of others, and of ourselves is premised within our story. Thus, I cannot escape the reality that my parents were divorced when I was five years old and that I spent a great majority of my childhood/youth/young adulthood searching for my "idealized" father—the father I could imagine but was never present to me.

The shape of a narrative will be determined by the beliefs one brings to it. Our personal narratives have multiple plots; our stories are connected to places. Human stories are constructed within the context of groups or communities of persons in time and in history. They are socially and historically conditioned (cf. the Western progress myth or the "American dream"). Stories draw on the resources of a particular person's community in the context of the social structures and institutions of which one is a part. So, again, my story is not only influenced by the fact that my parents were divorced, but also by the fact that, while I had one very absent father, I functionally had four mothers (and yes, one is enough). I grew up in rural northeastern Ohio, in the home of my maternal grandparents, with two of my aunts living right down the street. All of this is inevitably a part of the person I have become.

What Story? Whose Story? The Practice of Deception

Our focus here is on the texture of narrative, the reality of storied living, the art of storytelling and story-hearing, the mystery of the story, grand stories, even God's grand story. We are alive at a time when grand narratives have come under forceful critique, particularly in relationship to questions of truth. There is good reason for such critique when claims of truthfulness for any narrative are based on power and privilege rather than participation in a grand conversation to which all people are invited and have access. We are also susceptible to the modernization of story, which itself is a kind of privilege: that "we should have no story but the story we chose when we had no story, which we call freedom."[1] To the contrary, there are stories that we do not choose; they come to us as gift. The Christian claim is that we are creatures who have been made part of a larger story—God's story—into which we have been grafted as a gracious act of love. We receive this gift and join this story as participant rather than author, as sojourner rather than owner.

Every child, every person, is and will be shaped by some story, inherent to which are values and beliefs. A family cannot not teach and pass on values and beliefs about life and the world and other people. What stories and whose values are to be passed on? From whence do our stories come? What is their source? These are questions that need to be asked.

Can you begin to see where this is leading? As human beings we use what is available to us in constructing narratives, in the telling of our stories. For instance, our stories will be influenced by gender and, within Western, industrialized cultures, influenced by individualism and consumerism. Our narratives reflect the way we are positioned in society. Different communities will privilege different discourses or narratives. There is a certain kind of discourse privileged in a place like a seminary, namely, academese or semanese. This is also how various forms of slang become accepted and widely used, for instance, in youth cultures where talking the right language is like learning a code that leads to privilege. Human beings "perform"; we do what we know and say. Our narratives can themselves become a covert and even overt form of social control.

Human beings are storied people; we live storied lives. We are also masters of deception, including self-deception, which creates the illusion that one is in control not only of oneself but of others, as well. We do this individually and collectively or socially. Illusory attempts to control others quickly leads to what Martin Buber calls "I-it" rather than "I-thou" relationships.[2] An "I-it" relationship marginalizes and objectifies another person or group or culture. An "I-thou" relationship affirms the value, worth, and dignity of the other. Human beings are deceived easily into believing that one story is privileged over another, that one is more important or more significant or even more interesting. This sense of privilege and the power differential it creates divides, marginalizes, and oppresses others. This is the story of human sin. This is our story, too.

Storied Waters: The Judeo-Christian Heritage and the Jesus Story

Human beings are ensnared within self-justifying impulses, self-love run amuck, and trusting what is not worthy of trust—all that the Christian faith calls "sin." Every person is called out of this egocentric lifestyle by God's forgiving and liberating Word and toward a different vision of being human. At the heart of God's story is the gift of being chosen, addressed, and called out because God so chooses: "Once you were not a people, but now you are God's people; once you had not received mercy, but now you have received mercy" (1 Peter 2:10).

The Christian practice of baptism is more than a holy ritual or religiously sanctioned rite of passage. Baptism ushers a person into the story of God's love revealed in Jesus Christ:

> But when the goodness and loving-kindness of God our Savior appeared, [God] saved us, not because of any works of righteousness that we had done, but according to [God's] mercy, through the water of rebirth and renewal by the Holy Spirit. This Spirit [God] poured out on us richly through Jesus Christ our Savior, so that, having been justified by his grace, we might become heirs according to the hope of eternal life (Titus 3:4-7).

To be baptized is to be plunged into God's grand story—the entire biblical story and, in particular, the story of the life, death, and resurrection of Jesus Christ. The waters of baptism are *storied waters.*[3] At the center of this radical, alternative story is the new reality that Jesus ushered in—the reign of God. The reign of God is a reality where:

All is gift
God alone is God
There is forgiveness for all

All people are precious
Enemies are loved and strangers and outcasts are welcomed
There is hope for the future
God's food is for all
The last are first and the first are last
All people and all creation have dignity
Sin, death, and evil are defeated
Jesus is with us always
There is promise of resurrection the Holy Spirit is teacher and guide.
And all human distinctions and divisions have ended because . . .
"There is no longer Jew or Greek, slave or free, male or female; for
we are all one in Christ Jesus" (Gal. 3:28).[4]

It is this story that is addressed to us as gospel; it is this story
that we hear as gospel; it is this story that we are called to speak as
gospel; it is this story that we seek to live as gospel. As the people
of God we are called to be servants of God's story, the story of the
triune God of the Hebrew and Christian Scriptures, the "story of
Israel and its Jesus, told as a message of final destiny." This is not
only the "God who raised Israel's Jesus from the dead," but also God
as the one who in the Spirit of the resurrected Jesus bears death into
God's very being.[5]

In the baptismal newness of each new day we have the foundation from which to constantly examine our own practices of storied
living. The central Christian practices of Eucharist and confession/
absolution foster such ongoing examination. The Holy Spirit invites
us, opens us, and challenges us to deconstruct narratives (stories)
that privilege our use of power or place over against others. The
story of God, at the heart of which is the inbreaking of the reign of
God in Jesus Christ, exposes our involvement in institutional/soci-
etal oppression. The church, the gathered community of God, the
body of Christ, is itself subject to distortions. Through the *viva vox
evangellii* (the living voice of the gospel), the Holy Spirit reveals our

collective attempts to establish new idols or dividing practices. The story of the inbreaking of God's reign is a convicting and liberating story in the midst of all human attempts to dominate, domesticate, and divide.

The Practice of Dwelling in the Story

At the core of story-hearing and storytelling is a relationship. The hearing and telling of stories inevitably involves attending to a relationship, again, in Buber's words, as an "I-thou" rather than an "I-it" relationship. There can be no privileging of a particular person's story over another—nor any group or nation—as more important or more significant or even more interesting. There are at least *three practices of story* that can help us love and serve God and neighbor as the people of God in God's world rather than inside the church.

Simply put, we are called to *dwell in God's story:* to read and study, pray and ponder the Scriptures. As the people of God, our lives are set within a different story that narrates an alternative vision for the life and future of the world. God's story sets us on a journey—a mission journey—that calls us out beyond ourselves, beyond our congregations, and beyond our cozy confines. One word that the New Testament commonly uses for church is translated from the Greek word *ekklesia,* which comes from two words: *ek,* meaning "out," and *kaleo,* meaning "to call." To be the people of God is to be called out on a mission journey, a journey on which we are all God-spotters. This is where the adventure kicks into high gear—tracking the Holy Spirit, picking up the scent of the sacred, looking for the reign of God to pop up like a daisy through the crack in the sidewalk so that we can point to it, shout with joy to all who would hear, celebrate with all who would sing and dance and spin, and stoke the flames of the Spirit. The practice of dwelling in God's story locates and centers us in response to the question, "Who are we?" We are a people of the Way, a people on the Way.

The question, "Who am I?" is the correlate to the question, "Who are we?" and both are basic human questions. Both questions, the individual and the corporate, are critical leadership questions, as well. They are questions of ongoing discernment, and they need to be asked regularly and deliberately. They also are questions that deserve an honest response because they are, at root, sacred questions. But they also are difficult, potentially painful, and confusing questions that people are want to avoid.

Claiming Our True Identities as People of God

During the 1997–1998 academic year I lived in the Twin Cities of Minneapolis and St. Paul and served as a pastor at a large suburban congregation while finishing my dissertation and teaching at Luther Seminary as a sabbatical replacement—a light middleweight theological hired hand. Due to a strange set of circumstances that year, I also ended up as a candidate for faculty position at the seminary—a position that included the two core courses I happened to be teaching. It was a long search process, in the middle of which was a span of some four months when there was little communication between the institution and the candidates. It was, to say the least, an awkward situation. I felt as though I was constantly being observed and evaluated, and, to some extent, I was probably was.

It felt less like life in the proverbial fish bowl and more like life in a glass pressure cooker. I was continually on edge, performing, pretending, and basically trying to please people, though I didn't exactly know whom. Instead of trying to discover what kind of teacher I could best be at that particular juncture in my life, I spent an enormous amount of time and energy trying to figure out how to teach so that I could fit in and get the job. I constantly second-guessed everything I said or did. I was, shall we say, not a very effective teacher. I began to dread going to my classes. It was a stifling way to live.

I was delivered from this teacher-as-poser lifestyle, at least for a moment, one evening late in the winter quarter. I remember the day clearly. I had a funeral in the early afternoon, and then headed back over to Luther, still in full, black clergy dress, including a pectoral cross I often wore. I lectured the second hour. As usual, it felt brutal, and I felt sorry for the students.

As soon as the hour ended, the students scooped up their coats and books and quickly left. I intended to do the same, stuffing papers in my satchel and gathering up my books. It took me a moment to realize that Tom had not left. He was still sitting in his seat in the front row where he had been the entire class. When I looked up and noticed him, I hardly had time to say anything before he was standing in front of me. He was close to me. My internal alarm was going off, "Personal space breached. Personal space breached."

Tom put his index finger in the middle of the pectoral cross I was wearing and pushed—pretty hard, actually. "Claim your baptism," he said. "You are a free man in Christ." He pushed his finger into the cross a bit harder, then backed away and quickly left the room.

I was stunned. I sat back onto the stool behind me. Tears were streaming down my face. My chest hurt a bit. I looked down, inside my shirt, and could see that the cross had left an imprint, however faint, on my sternum. The word he spoke to me was so terse, so direct, so liberating, that I didn't exactly know what to do with it, though I had the sense that I desperately needed to hear it. I still struggle, of course, with the temptation to perform, to pretend, to want to please—in short, to be someone other than who I am. But that night I was reminded, but for a moment, wherein lies my true identity.

One of the most significant theological legacies of Martin Luther is found in his insight that "justification by works of the law leads to death."[6] As the people of God, we need to be reminded, both individually and corporately, who we are from a theological perspective. We are first and foremost who God declares us to be: forgiven sinners, valued and valuable, beloved of the Lord, called to join in God's mission of love and mercy in Christ. The theological correlate is justification. It is the gift and calling of God's people to bear this word of hope and promise. But it is not our word; it is God's word, given as a gift. It is both the privilege and responsibility of the whole people of God to declare this word. But we must hear this word, dwell in this word in order to declare it. We must keep asking, time and time again, as honestly and authentically as possible, how we are called to bear witness to Christ as the people of God.

It is disconcerting, to say the least, how often and easily we tend to forget that we have passed through storied waters, and that the love of the Holy One in whose name we are claimed and baptized has left a mark imprinted on us, water and ashes the same mark. And I daresay that it is equally as disconcerting how often and easily all of the baptized, even and especially in our churches, are tempted to forget the same. There is so often such a thin distance between people in our congregations and communities that keep us from genuinely and honestly meeting, on occasion, as human beings, without pretense or fear, to talk about this shared journey. This is the journey that counts—from birth through baptism to burial and resurrection.

Israel passed through the waters and stumbled, and murmured and wandered for forty years in a wilderness. It was a place of struggle and confusion and, of course, apostasy. It was a place of questioning: "Is God with us or not? Who are we to be as the people of God?" In time, there came another passing through waters, this one Son of God passing through the waters of baptism. The same Spirit that descended on Jesus after he passed through the waters drove him into his own wilderness. There Jesus had to discover what kind of messiah he would be, or not be. There Jesus was tested for forty days by Satan and offered some tempting choices, in many ways the

classic alternatives to an identity faithful to God: to satiate the needs
of the body, to avoid suffering, the appeal of unbridled power. In the
face of these powerful alternatives, Jesus clung to the word of God.

Jesus chose and followed a singular path. Even now, the people
of God, having passed through the waters with him, walk in his
shadow. Only in Christ can we discover who we are truly called to
be. Only in Christ can we make this journey together.

In the letters of Flannery O'Connor, there is a story that began
as *A Memoir of Mary Ann.* It is a story about a young girl who
frequently visits a convent and the sisters who live there. She loves
going there, but every time she arrives and every time she leaves, a
particular sister gives her a hug, and the crucifix on the sister's belt is
pressed into this young girl's cheek. This gesture of love, O'Connor
writes, always leaves a mark.[7]

On our journey from baptism through burial toward the resurrection, we need be reminded often of our true identity. It is God's
story that bears this word of hope and promise about our true identity. "Who am I?" A daughter or son of God. "Who are we?" The
people of God. It is a privilege and responsibility that we all share,
to remind one another who we are and the vocation to which we are
called. And that vocation, the calling of all of us, is the calling to be
Christs in the world.

The Practice of Story-Hearing

The *second story practice* is that of story-hearing—serving as
listener and observer, paying attention to and listening to the stories of others. Listening is important, profoundly important. It is
increasingly significant at a time when so many people suffer from
perpetual information overload. As the people of God, we understand the practice of listening as a way to meet one another, to honor
and respect another person and his or her story, to foster a healthy
and genuine relationship. We also understand the importance of
listening in order to help others discover and begin to use their gifts

and passion in ministry. Finally, we recognize that an essential skill of effective pastoral leadership is the ability to help others interpret their own experiences and stories within the context of the over-arching story of God's redemptive history. Christian leaders (and that's all of the baptized) are able to tell God's grand story because they listen and are then able to make the connection between God's story and the stories of others.

At the turn of this new millennium, I inhabited a cubby at the Lutheran Center in Chicago while serving on the ELCA Youth Ministries/Gathering team. In the run-up to the 2000 ELCA Youth Gathering in St. Louis, I traveled from Chicago to St. Louis countless times. My favorite place to stay was the Omni Hotel—a quaint, historic, downtown property. Over the course of many long weekends at the Omni, I became acquainted with Leslie. A mostly full-time community college student, she worked the second shift behind the front desk at the hotel and generally was working when I checked in.

Our conversation during the check-in process was fairly polite, brief, and chatty. In late June 2000, I arrived in St. Louis and checked into the Omni for a much longer stay that included both weeks of the youth gathering. This time our chitchat quickly turned into more of a conversation. Leslie was aware that thousands of teenagers would soon descend upon her city and that somehow I was connected to this massive gathering.

So she began to ask questions. "Now, you work for a church, right?"

"Yes, I work for a large denomination, the Evangelical Lutheran Church in America."

"So these are church kids coming for this youth gathering?"

"Yep, mostly Lutheran church kids coming with adult leaders from all over the country and even some from around the world."

"Yeah? I was Lutheran growing up. So . . . I know you've told me this, but why exactly are they coming here to St. Louis? What are they going to do?"

"As I've said, they are coming to St. Louis for a youth gathering."

I did my best to answer her questions and so on and so forth. The point is that our conversation had moved from chitchat to something more this time. There was a pause, a lull in our conversation, so I took a risk. I figured that since she was curious and had asked me some questions, I could do the same. "So what about you, Leslie? You said that you grew up Lutheran. What about now? Are you interested in God? Are you a part of a church community?"

She shut down. It was as if that was the last question in the world she had wanted someone to ask. I quickly picked up on her unspoken signals; only an idiot could have missed the fact that I had stepped over some intangible, invisible but nonetheless real boundary. So I quickly retreated. "No offense intended," I said. "I was merely curious. I figured we were having a conversation and I could ask questions too. Really . . . just curious."

The look that had galvanized on her face asked me if I was serious. Was I really curious? Did I really want to know that about her? My look in response said, yes. "I'm Wiccan," she said emphatically. My immediate, reflexive and hopefully genuine response was to say, "Really . . ." and before I could say anything else she said, "Really! You got a problem with that?"

"No," I said, "no problem. It's just that I don't know much about what it means to be Wiccan, and I'm not sure that I've ever talked with someone who does. Most of what I do know is probably based on misconceptions and stereotypes. I'd like to hear your story and learn more about it, that's all."

Once again she looked at me, eyes blazing, jaw firmly set, as if to ask if I was serious about wanting to learn more. I returned the look, a bit more kindly I'd like to think, as if to say that indeed I really would like to hear her story and learn more. "I'm finished here at 11:00 P.M.," she said. "If you're serious, be here at 11:05 and you can buy me a coffee. Then we'll see."

I returned to the hotel lobby shortly after 11:00 P.M. She was waiting. We took a table right by the entry to the hotel restaurant, sat down, and ordered our drinks. There was an awkward silence at first, as if we didn't quite know how to pick up the conversation. I tried to make a go at it, at which point she said, quite directly, "Listen, I've been beat up (figuratively speaking) by Christians more than you can imagine over the years when I've talked about my religious preference. So I've stopped talking about it. Point is, I can smell manipulation a mile away, so don't even try it."

I assured her that I intended no manipulation. After a bit, she began to speak. Forty-five minutes later she was still talking when she glanced at her watch, amazed at how much time had passed. I had been listening, for which she was grateful, she said, quickly apologizing for talking so much. I told her I didn't mind. I had learned a lot and thought her story was pretty interesting, albeit painful from her perspective.

"What about you?" she said. "What's your story? I like stories, so let's hear it." So I proceeded to tell her my story. I told her about my family and my work and my childhood and my friends. I told her about how the God whose face was set toward the world in Jesus had found me through the witness of some kindly people at a small country church in rural northeastern Ohio. Being found by my God had made all the difference in my life, I said, and in the life of the world as well, I believed. It was her turn to listen, and listen she did. Soon it was close to 1:00 A.M. It was late and we were tired, but this I know: I had participated in a safe, sane, respectful conversation with another human being that was, at its core, deeply evangelical.

The Practice of Storytelling and Telling the Story

Telling the story is best accomplished through the use of stories, but they are not the same thing. Christian leaders aspire not to some idealized prototype of the funny, charismatic, and, at just the right moment, moving storyteller, but to tell God's story—the great biblical Genesis to Revelation story. God's story is the narrative backdrop, the primary reference point for all of our little stories. We tell God's story not as experts or professionals, but out of the depths and riches of our own life with God, using our own language of faith. This will gain much more traction than any well-rehearsed, polished shtick. Authentic Christian communication happens in light of the whole story of what God has promised to do, has done, and is doing, and from the perspective of the theological tradition of which we are a part.

There is no doubt that stories are the primary currency for communicating in emerging cultures today. Writing for the Young Leaders Network a few years ago, Brian McLaren identified three reasons why the story is a compelling mode of communication: stories invite participation, stories are sneaky, and the story is the point. About stories being sneaky he writes:

> A story doesn't grab you by the lapels and bring you close so that you can smell the garlic and coffee and Altoids on the breath. What a story does is sneak up behind you and whisper something in your ear. And when you turn around to see what it is, it kicks you in the butt and runs and hides behind a bush. And in so doing, a story does something that no abstract proposition can ever do. It stops you in your tracks and makes you think. It catches your attention and won't let go. You can't help it. A story can't be argued with or dismissed like a proposition. A story is just sneaky. It doesn't teach by induction or deduction. It teaches by abduction. It abducts your attention and it won't let you go until you have done some thinking for yourself.[8]

The challenge for missional, Christian leaders communicating in the emerging culture is to dwell in God's Word and listen to the stories of others before using the wonderful benefits of storytelling to tell God's grand story. Although the practice of *martyreo* (bearing witness) is central to evangelical living, there is one important caveat: In our emerging cultural context today, one must earn the right to speak the good news of Jesus Christ to another. This does not mean that we do not speak, but that we must first be patient and listen in order to speak credibly and intelligibly. Evangelical living begins with evangelical listening, that is, being present and attending to others in such a way as to build trust and lead people to deeper faith questions. This approach takes time and patience; there is no model or magic formulae. This is a challenge for all of us who live in the age of the quick fix.

Our calling as church in the emerging culture is not to "do" evangelism, but to "live" kingdom—practicing faith and serving the reign of God as disciples of Jesus—and along the way inviting others into living the same. This is what we see happening between Philip and the Ethiopian eunuch in Acts 8. So, hallelujah! Evangelism is not our business! The notion perpetuated by the modern church (both in its mainline and evangelical expressions) that evangelism is in any way a task of the church has led the church to expend critical missional energy going up a down staircase, shouldering a burden church cannot bear and a weight church cannot carry.

Evangelism is the work of the Holy Spirit. This recognizing is grace, and it will free the church to venture "post-evangelism" into communal and individual participation in the *missio Dei*. In many church communities the focus is on *being* evangelical rather than doing evangelism. In fact, as soon as evangelism becomes something that one must "do," we risk losing touch with the evangelical impulse that is central to the Christian gospel.

God intends Christianity to be more than a system of belief or a commodity that can be programmed, packaged, and marketed as the ever-elusive new and improved quick fix. Christian beliefs and practices are intended to foster a way of life as followers of Jesus Christ that in turn send us into the world to imitate the forgiveness, mercy, and love of God. Drawn by the Spirit, our cause and deepest passion is to attend to the reign of God within community and in God's world. Community in Jesus Christ is not something we create or can coerce people into—it is a gift to which the Spirit calls people. In an authentic Christian community there are no insiders and outsiders, but only souls from both far off and nearby being drawn closer to God and one another by the love of Christ.

Church communities are called to foster practices of evangelical living and forego any programmatic, modernist attempts at "doing" evangelism. Figural practices that cultivate a posture of evangelical living include: attending or deeply listening to the stories of others; observing and paying attention to the embedded spirituality that exists in people's lives; and honoring and taking others seriously as persons, understanding that each person's spiritual path is unique.

There are challenges before us, no doubt—challenges that call us out of our private enclaves and comfort zones and into seemingly unorthodox, even "profane" settings. We can better immerse ourselves in particular contexts—cafés, music lounges, pubs—in order to set up "listening posts" where we can pay attention to, observe, listen, learn, befriend, and join in dialog with others. In so doing we will live into our identity as the people of God, cultivating Christ-centered relationships as we stand in between God's story and the stories of others around us.

The birthing of Christians is a work of the Holy Spirit, to which the church community is midwife. As people are called by the Holy Spirit into a love relationship with God, the people of God are called to come alongside them as they journey and discern a calling to the Christian faith. In the next chapter we're going to take a look at how some Christian communities are living God's mission and being church in today's emerging cultures.

Questions for Reflection & Discussion

1. What is your story? Share something from your own story that is fundamental to understanding who you are as a person.

2. What are the key stories, values, and beliefs that have been passed on to you? From whence did they come? What do you want to pass on to others?

3. What do you find most compelling in God's grand story—the entire biblical story and, in particular, the story of Jesus Christ?

4. Think about the following questions in terms of your own life as well as the Christian community to which you belong. How are you dwelling in God's story? How are you listening to and hearing the stories of others? How are you bearing witness to the triune God, speaking and being good news to others?

4

The Emerging Church:
Postmodern Worshiping
Communities or Emerging
Ecclesiologies?

Speaking a New Language

It seems as though to dress up anything churchy and make it new and improved these days we need to use some variation of the word *emerge*, generally emerging or emergent. So what's up with this? Is it merely the newest (at least for the time being), most interesting, and lucrative ecclesiastical fad—so many talking heads, so few conferences? Is it the most current and "with it" form of ecclesio-babble—like, everybody knows emerging church, dude? Is it a flashy foil over against which a really cool looking straw person has been set up, generating a dicey polemic for late-night Internet addicts (aka the blogosphere)? Maybe, maybe, and maybe. Or is all of this emerging theo-babble something more, something deeper, something more profoundly insightful about the contemporary situation in which churches find themselves? Call me the eternal optimist, but I'm hedging my bets and opting for the latter.

The operative question with which many people have been living for almost a decade now is this: the emerging church—postmodern worshiping communities or an emerging ecclesiology (better yet, emerging ecclesiologies)? The emerging church is language that has become increasingly common currency these days. What's behind the language? What are the more significant referents or indicators? Are there, in fact, emerging ways of understanding and being church that are lurking in the wings, on the ground, taken a hold, and changing the religious landscape?

Experiments—the so-called postmodern worshiping communities—have been popping up around the world, especially in the United Kingdom, the United States, Canada, South Africa, and Australia. The rate of proliferation is amazing: Search for the term "emerging churches" on the Internet and see what you get! Some are sponsored by churches and denominations while others are nondenominational or independent; many are Christian, some come from other religious traditions, and a few are still trying to decide. For the most part, I have been paying attention to those communities broadly characterized as Christian. Though the background for many of these Christian communities (and their leadership) is the modern evangelical denominational ethos, in reality they represent the "generous orthodoxy"[1] of the historic Christian faith. If these communities are denominationally linked, they live typically on the fringe of the denomination. Karen Ward, abbess of the Church of the Apostles in Seattle, has used the image of *dinghy* and *mother ship* to reflect the relationship between emerging church community and larger church body. Denominationally linked or not, many of these communities forge and maintain multiple ecclesiastical relationship—often expanding and redefining in practice more modern, conventional notions of ecumenism.[2]

Virtually all the communities in which I am interested have been birthed by people from the first postmodern generation (so-called Generation X) and colonized and cultivated by people from that generation as well as the next (the so-called Millennials).[3] This is not insignificant to the work of ministry. Many, so many, of the aforementioned people were groomed by some more conventional form of "the church" and eventually checked out in search of other forms of communal, religious life.

The language of the emerging church intends to be *descriptive, not prescriptive*—no "be like Mike" mentality here. In short, most emerging churches are particular subsets (communities) of Christians exercising theological imagination, not so much rethinking as re-living Christianity against the backdrop of postmodernism (for lack of a better phrase).

There are many superbly written, intellectually rigorous, honest, and insightful treatments of postmodernity, postmodernism, and postmodern cultures. Though often freely interchanged, these terms are not synonymous, so for our purposes here, I prefer to use the term *post-whateverism.*[4] What is post-whateverism? It's an interesting question, but it depends on whom you ask.[5] How's that for a post-whatever response?

Perhaps more than anything else, the language of post-whateverism refers to a concept of flux. In much, but not all of the world, people have been living in and through an age of massive transition between what was (the industrial age), what is (the infomedia age), and what is coming (the biotechnology age?). In the process, we are amateur cartographers trying to map and navigate the socio-political landscape of this emerging world. More to the point, we are trying to navigate this fluid landscape as people of faith with our once-inhabited churches more and more vacant and many up for sale.

Most significantly, transition has meant massive shifts. In the last few decades, major shifts in virtually every sphere of life have fundamentally changed the world as we knew it. In South Africa/Namibia it is before and after apartheid; in Germany and Eastern Europe, before and after "the wall"; in the United States, shifts defined by Vietnam and Watergate, Columbine and 9/11; in China, by Tiananmen Square. And seemingly everywhere the landscape has been altered, redefined by PCs, the Internet, and virtual technology.[6] The late Peter Drucker narrates well the way in which living through such shifting of the social tectonic plates can be a disjointing experience:

Every few hundred years in Western history there occurs a sharp transformation . . . within a few short decades, a society rear-ranges itself—its worldview; its basic values; its social and political structure; its arts; its key institutions. . . . . Fifty years later, there is a new world and the people born then cannot even imagine the world in which their grandparents lived and into which their own parents were born. We are currently living through just such a transformation.[7]

Regardless of whether one defines post-whateverism in a Websteresque manner ("a complex set of reactions to modern philosophy and its presumptions") or more in terms of common parlance (the long dry reign of rationalism is over), the massive transition to which the language of post-whateverism refers has two seeds. The first seed, to which the aforementioned definitions tipped the hat, is an increasingly pervasive disenchantment with Enlightenment dogma.[8] The second seed of the transition is an emerging global culture or, in common parlance, a big world moving faster, getting smaller, and coming closer all the time. Those born after 1940 stood at the edge of the water, sniffed the ocean breeze, and experienced the first winds of the coming change. Those born after 1960 heard the cry, "Surf's up!" and braved the waves of change. They are the ones presently building the first huts on the beach of the future. But it will be those born after 1980 who will be the first settlers, moving inland and constructing a more lasting homestead in the new world.

The world of today is caught in the crack between what was and what is emerging. This crack began opening in 1960 and will close sometime around the year 2014. Trusted values held for centu-ries are falling into this crack, never to be seen again. Ideas and methodologies that once worked no longer achieve the desired results. This crack in our history is so enormous that it is causing a metamorphosis in every area of life. . . . Today, the fastest way to fail is to improve on yesterday's successes.[9]

The point of this minor foray into post-whateverism is that definitions are slippery, and we have been and are in the midst of what Graham Ward calls a "cultural sea change." The churches—the people of God—are standing on cultural and social tectonic plates that are shifting underneath. We are trying to find our land legs so that we can navigate this fluid, emerging landscape during a time of transition.

Seeking to Describe the Emerging Church

I was invited recently to participate in a theological conference entitled, "Church at the Cross Road: The Emerging Church." When I first saw the flyer advertising the conference I immediately thought, "Yes! They've got it right." The conundrum in which we (the churches) find ourselves today is at its core a *missional* and *ecclesiological* challenge. What does it mean for the *church* to *be church* today? This seems to be the most urgent question. Emerging church communities are attempting to live this question, thereby resisting the temptation to allow it to remain simply a good question. These communities also are resisting the temptation to create more or new rules whereby navigation might come easier. Rather, emerging church communities are doing the poetic work of re-narrating the religious landscape; they are producing new stories, an outgrowth of their willingness to practice faithful innovation. In a time of transition, can the church live in a tension: moored to our collective past as the people of God and yet freed to experiment and take risks for the reign of God?

So in typical post-whatever fashion, here first is what the emerging church is *not*. It is not the mega-church "model" nor the church growth approach nor contemporary worship nor generational ministry (whatever that is). It is not prescriptive; that is, it is not intended to be a mold, model, or formulae that others simply need to figure out how to "tweak," or, at worst, replicate and adopt (not to be confused with adapt, because adaptive rather than adoptive work actually can become culturally authentic even if it is not indigenous to a particular community). The emerging church is cultivating communities of faithful innovation that are seeking to navigate the postmodern cultural landscape closely tethered to God's story.

These communities are not only asking but seeking to live an operative question: What does it mean to be *who we are where we are?* This question shines the light on two huge aspects of a people's life together in community: *identity* and *geography* (location). Intentional, sustained attention to who we are and where we are spawn communal conversation and critical reflection that become part of the air that is breathed. People not only come to accept it; they expect it as well. The question is never answered; it is continually, even relentlessly pursued, and thus mitigates against complacency. This process can keep a community honest and on edge, fostering openness and curiosity. Whatever their origins, common principles and practices are noticeable as many emerging church communities seek to live this question.

So what distinguishes emerging church communities from more conventional churches? This is a question about which many people are curious and to which many others are seeking to respond, myself included. Common principles and practices are shared by a wide variety of emerging church communities. A caveat before we continue: the principles and practices noted here are based more on informal rather than formal research. I do not participate nor lead in an emerging church community. Rather, I consider myself a curious and (hopefully) careful observer. In other words, these suggestions are based on observations made and conversations joined over the past six years or so while intentionally visiting a wide variety of emerging church communities (along with keeping abreast of the emerging church conversation via the current literature being produced, including blogs and e-zines—some of which are listed in the Additional Resources section of this book). Nonetheless, what is suggested here are not abstractions. The following twenty-two observations are based on current practices of ministry in light of what is actually taking place in communities of faith planted, cultivated, and populated mostly, but not exclusively by a new wave of missional, Christian leaders with bold, creative, and fairly orthodox sensibilities about what it means to be church in a culturally authentic manner.

1. Worship = team design

Worship is designed, planned, and led by a team. This is not a group of people such as the garden-variety worship committee that fills in the blanks (at best picking hymns, at worst rubber-stamping what the staff has already chosen) for worship. Rather, this is an ongoing, weekly process wherein people with various gifts and expertise—music, the arts, poetry, graphic design, audio/video technology—engage in the design and implementation of worship on behalf of and as the community. Participation in such an organic process depends not on title or status but on role and gift, which means that ordained persons may or may not be on the team. Such a process that births a communal worship gathering each week (at least) demands deliberate, open, fluid, and ongoing communication.

2. Feedback loops

Feedback loops become a critical component of communal life and culture. Continuous feedback loops foster needed, ongoing communication and serve to critique and inform planning in the community. Certain elements may be used repeatedly in the weekly, communal worship gathering. In other words, there may be, and most often is, a kind of embedded *Ordo*.[10] On the other hand, there is also room for spontaneity so that worship can be sculpted and tailored to fit the life of a community in a given time and place (some might call this contextualizing the worship experience). This sculpting or tailoring can be called forth by a variety of factors—the assigned or chosen biblical text(s), the rhythm of the saints (liturgical calendar), or something specific to the life of a given community. This is the best of what liturgy means: working out from an ordo and sculpting the worship experience to fit the life of a community. At the extreme, the worship experience is new each week; at the least, the worship experience is, to some degree, unique each week.

3. The arts are back

After a long hiatus from particularly Protestant worship, the arts are back. Art is more than a banner hanging in the sanctuary or a series of beautiful stained-glass windows (though these are certainly artistic expressions). In many emerging church communities, the arts—often, if not mostly generated locally—are used extensively, including painting, sculpture, graphics, poetry, drama, dance, and ritual movement.[11] The arts are employed not only extensively, but figurally as well. In other words, they are more than window dressing; they are portals to holy things and expressions of faithful questing and questioning. For many people, the arts provide non-discursive,[12] non-linear expressions of thoughts, feelings, questions, and imagination.

4. Language matters

Language is a key issue in emerging church communities, and narrative is the common currency. The emphasis is on "real" experiences, and words and stories are the primary vehicle. You won't hear canned sermon illustrations or the rereading of trite forwarded e-mails in these settings. Story—both telling God's story and story-telling—plays a central role in the life of the community.

The telling and hearing of stories is foregrounded in the life of the community. Rote, wooden, churchy language is seldom employed, and conceptual or theoretical descriptions as a starting point are suspect. If or when such language is used, it often evokes immediate suspicion and is generally ignored. There is an aversion to this kind of language, not only because it often feels and sounds inauthentic, but also because it easily becomes code language and is inaccessible to so many people. Stories are anything but inaccessible; they are universal and transcultural—everyone has them, needs to tell them, and wants to be heard. Leaders listen carefully to stories and use them for the ongoing, poetic work of narrating the life together of a people.

5. Room for spontaneity

The necessary tension between spontaneity and structure was noted earlier with regard to the worship gathering. Worship is ordered but not over-defined nor over-prescribed, which means creating or, better yet, leaving space for spontaneity. For instance, meanings are found (and welcome) that were not anticipated by the "planners" or "leaders," and these alternative meanings feed the ongoing conversation of the community. This tension is not something that can be controlled, but rather a dynamic within which we must live. Theologically, spontaneity is the domain of the Holy Spirit, and this makes a lot of Christians nervous, strange as that might sound. Why so? Because it is risky and reminds us that ultimately we are not in control. The Scriptures are rife with stories about the Holy Spirit that ought to make Christ followers nervous. The Holy Spirit is mediated in and through the community, which can guard against any attempt to domesticate God's Spirit and keep a community open to that which ultimately comes from outside of us: the transformational love and power of God in Jesus Christ.

6. Music at the core

Music is one of the most indigenous elements of emerging church communities. Though most emerging church experiments thus far use a "rock" idiom, other musical genres—Celtic, Taize, Gregorian chant or a techno club-vibe are also used. More significant than the particular idiom is the fact that much of the music comes from within the community. And the musicians are not the only ones who produce the music of the community. Back-room poets and those who keep journals are just as apt to craft text for song as those who sing and play the instruments. There is a principle at work here: music grows out of an authentic experience of God within community. Many emerging church communities risk creating new musical styles that serve old texts, and employing old musical styles that serve new texts. Either way there is a deep mining of the great Christian tradition, within a particular community, and in relationship to that community's life together with God. Music has, and creates an affect; it is deeply soulful and can connect with people emotionally without lapsing into emotionalism. It is one of the primary vehicles by which people offer praise and voice lament.

7. Worship space and time

For the longest time, the banner on my cell phone read, "God is here." It served as an important daily reminder: Wherever you go, there is God. In other words, though there might be places that feel or appear to be God-forsaken, there are no God-less places, which is to say, there is no thing or no place or no space beyond the reach of the transformational power and love of God in Christ Jesus. Now, this is a rather significant theological claim. It is a claim rooted in God's utter identification with sinners in the crucifixion of Jesus Christ and God's ultimate defeat of all that would separate human beings and a broken creation from God in the resurrection and ascension of Jesus Christ. It is also a claim that refuses to remain a theological abstraction.

Many emerging church communities will gather in an intentionally "profane"[13] setting, the kind of place that many people (Christians included) would write off as God-forsaken. Why? Oftentimes because a space like an old theatre or an abandoned warehouse is vacant and needs an occupant. Certainly not to "take God" into such a setting the way that some Christians talk about "taking God or prayer into the public schools." To the contrary, the purpose is to bear witness to a God who, in Christ, has placed a lasting claim on all of creation. The distinction between the sacred and the secular is a false distinction, at least to the extent that we still believe in the First Article of the great creeds of the church, for instance. Everything "in heaven and on earth" belongs to God, it has all been claimed by God, and in the future that God has promised the whole creation will be renewed and transformed.

So in many emerging church contexts the space and time for the worship gathering are typically not "traditional" in the sense of conventional. Part of the process of community formation involves creating a sacred space and time that fits into the natural rhythm of the people's lives. The worship gathering is often, but not always, on Saturday or Sunday evenings. When asked, "Why Saturday or Sunday evening?" people will often respond to the question with another question: "Honestly, do you really like getting up early on Sunday morning to go to worship?" Many people would rather rise leisurely (read: sleep late), cook a big breakfast, read the paper, take a walk, play a game with the kids or visit friends or relatives, take a nap, and then gather in community for worship—for as long as it takes.

8. The function of humor

In emerging church communities, humor is expected, natural, and naturally used. In fact, the natural use of humor is part of what allows for and makes room for the spontaneity mentioned earlier. There are times when it is difficult to distinguish between preaching and a stand-up comedy act. On the one hand, the natural and appropriate use of humor is part of the air that the people breathe, and it functions to keep the community relaxed and receptive to what is being communicated. On the other hand, it easily can become leader-centric, a kind of cult-of-personality that centers on the main act, that had better deliver. Have you seen the movie, *Keeping the Faith?* This is intended at best as analogy, not comparison and certainly not example. Consider this excerpt from the film:

> Father Brian Kilkenney Finn: "The seven deadly sins. Who can name the seven deadly sins?" (No response) "People! It was a very popular film with Brad Pitt. You have the ultimate Cliff Note."[14]

9. Attention to texts

There is a rich and ample understanding of text that includes a full range of referentiality. Here text means both sacred text (the Bible, creeds) and cultural text (film, poetry). Emerging church communities take cultural texts as seriously as they take sacred texts, though cultural texts do not norm their belief and proclamation the way the Judeo-Christian Scriptures do. There is an extensive use of a variety of texts from pop culture, including allusions to television, film, music, video, and current literature, because often these mediums expose the profound questions with which people live and reflect the spiritual questing inherent in the human predicament. Leadership aims to help the community stand in front of the text and attend carefully, often critically to interpretation through dialog and discernment. This is just as apt to happen in the worship gathering as in a house church gathering. Multiple interpretations are expected and sought, with the express goal of helping people seek an authentic experience of God in community.

10. The understanding of suffering

In emerging church communities, suffering is acknowledged as a fundamental and unavoidable dimension of human life in the world. On the surface this might sound obvious enough: Well, duh, you would have to be either kidding yourself or asleep to deny the reality of suffering in the world. Yet folk wisdom, pop psychologies, and theologies of glory abound that seek to skirt or avoid or explain away the issue. You shouldn't complain, some would say. Those poor people in _____ (fill in the blank) have it so much worse. Or how about this one: People who suffer deserve it; they bring it on themselves. Here's one of my favorites: If you prayed harder or had more faith then you wouldn't suffer as much. Sure, there might be a kernel of truth in all of these would be "explanations" for suffering. Okay, maybe not the last one. Regardless, the point isn't to quibble about the cause of suffering. In emerging church communities, suffering simply is, and it is personal, social, and environmental.

What we can learn from many of these communities is how to live with the reality of suffering. Suffering is viewed as something to be joined, even befriended, rather than conquered or fixed. The suffering of others, both near and far, is something to be shared because the sharing of suffering mirrors the very life of God. Perhaps no biblical text says it so well and so eloquently as Hebrews 2:10: "It was fitting that God, for whom and through whom all things exist, in bringing many children to glory, should make the pioneer of their salvation perfect through sufferings." We live in a world that is in "bondage to decay" and "groaning in travail" (images from the eighth chapter of Romans). Though the world has come apart at the seams, God has sewn it together with the needle of the cross and the thread of a suffering love. To use a Lutheran theological category, sharing in the suffering of others is living the theology of the cross in community.

11. Experimentation and innovation

Emerging church communities are not afraid to experiment and embrace the practice of faithful innovation. Once again, the essential premise is that during periods of significant transition, people need not more rules, but more stories. Alternative approaches or practices that fit the ethos of a particular community will generate new stories and allow people to seek an authentic experience of God within community. This is not a "whatever" approach to being the church—whatever works or whatever people want or whatever seems to be the current cool thing. However, there is an acute awareness that alternative approaches or practices are needed to function and intelligibly communicate the Christian message during epochal change. Oftentimes, perhaps even most of the time, these approaches or practices represent nothing new, but rather a retrieval of the very old. My good friend and colleague Karen Ward, pastor at Church of the Apostles in the Fremont neighborhood of Seattle, calls this "ecclesiastical Dumpster-diving." It is deep mining of the great Christian tradition, reclaiming ancient values and practices and contextualizing them in a community for a new day. So, in the life of the community, the value might be that worship practices are more experiential and participatory. The goal would be for people to seek "full, active, and conscious" participation in a complete spiritual and physical sense. The practice could be communal *lectio divina*[15] rather than listening to one person read the text; walking a prayer labyrinth during the time for intercessory prayer rather than the appointed pray-er leading a prayer-and-response approach.

12. Statement of faith

A statement of faith is usually prominent and figural in the life of many emerging church communities. In and of itself this is neither unusual nor unique; in other church circles this might be called a mission or vision statement. What is interesting is that in many emerging church communities the statement of faith is increasingly one of the ancient creeds from the great tradition of the church (typically the Apostles' or Nicene)[16] I've heard a rationale for this best explained in the form of a question: "Why create a 'mission' or 'vision' statement when we have been gifted with a statement that has weathered many storms and defined the core beliefs of the one, holy, catholic, apostolic church throughout the ages?" Instead of putting their time and energy into continually creating a "mission," these communities receive the creeds as a gift, commit to joining the mission of God that the creeds articulate, and put their time, energy, and creativity toward living into these beliefs as their part in God's mission in the world. Vision becomes the discerning and living of mission as a particular community and in a particular neighborhood and locale. Functionally, these creedal statements serve as lodestar[17] rather than litmus test. Indeed, the creed as statement of faith serves as the primary gauge (rather than the pastor or the board or council) against which the community measures an idea or proposal or opportunity: "Does (fill in whatever) fit within the historic Christian faith expressed in the creed?" The point is that the creedal statement becomes the guiding light for the community—that to which people aspire in the living of their faith—rather than a system of belief to which one must agree in order to get in the door.

13. Genuine appreciation of diversity

There appears to be a genuine appreciation of diversity in many emerging church communities, not only in theory but also in practice. In these instances, the welcoming of diversity includes those more tangible categories one might expect—age, gender, race, economic status, and the like—as well as that which might be more intangible, such as appearance, opinions, and religious background (or, as is often the case, a lack of religious background or prior religious knowledge). The operative premise is that all human experience is valid, but not all human behavior is acceptable. People are welcomed "as they are" into a community wherein God's Spirit is the primary "glue" that holds them—blemishes and all—together in Christ. However, it needs to be said that diversity is not forced onto or into a community. In other words, these communities resist being diverse for the sake of being diverse. Emerging church communities seek to be open to the other and intentionally reach out to the diversity that is present in their neighborhood context. In order to do this, we must know who is in the community, which means proactive engagement in the lives of those in our "neighborhoods" and cultivating relationships through practices such as hospitality and listening.

14. Losing the labels

There is a genuine aversion to the use of broad, overarching labels in emerging church communities. It seems a popular communication pattern these days to use categories like "liberal" and "conservative" or "traditional" and "contemporary" to describe or define another person's preferences or point of view. The implication is that a category like "conservative" or "contemporary" can sum up a person's perspective—whether about religious belief, social issues, or political opinion. In reality, most human beings are more complicated than broad, simplistic categories and resist being defined by them.

In emerging church communities, such labels are regarded as wooden and useless, often stifling, and sometimes destructive. When used, these labels become "flags" that almost always are named and confronted directly. Why? Because labels generally function as conversation stoppers, and, as we shall see a bit later on, a fundamental value in many emerging church communities is open, mutual, and civil dialog. Labels are also dehumanizing. Think about it. How do you feel when someone slaps a label on you? When someone asks me, as happened recently on a plane trip, "So, are you a liberal or a conservative?" I cringe. "It depends," I want to say. "What do you mean by liberal and conservative? And what exactly are we talking about? Am I liberal or conservative about what? I'm fairly conservative when it comes to how we invest money toward our children's college education, but pretty liberal when it comes to how much peanut butter and jelly I use on my sandwiches."

Human beings are quirky creatures. It takes time and hard work to come to know and better understand another person. One of the practices that help emerging church communities honor the complexity of human social life is resisting broad, overarching categories and investing in listening and dialog. Sadly enough, the "emerging church" itself has become a label, merely another menu item on the great smorgasbord of church. If one needs a label for the "emerging church," I would suggest *"one, holy, catholic,* and *apostolic."*

15. Worship and/in community

Worship in emerging church communities seeks an authentic experience of God within community. There is a reciprocal relationship between these two realities—worship and community life. In other words, the community—not just a select few—produce worship, and this process of communal worship production creates broad-based ownership and investment and generates community. Worship grows out of and creates community. Community is understood on both a "macro" level, a corporate expression such as the worship gathering, and a "micro" level, as evidenced in rise of and return to the house church approach. There could be no commitment more significant in emerging church communities than the valuing of communal religious life over against the valuing of individual rights and preferences predominant in much of American Christianity. In this respect, many of these communities are rising to one of the critical challenges identified by Loren Mead some ten years ago: "The congregation is a community that lives in a community and is called to generate a sense of community."[18]

16. Robust doctrine of God

What is church? Church is the *trinitarian communitas,* the trinitarian community. British academic Pete Ward argues, in a decidedly theological manner, that church is "a series of relationships and connections in Christ."[19]

> The church is formed and shaped by God. This theological truth must condition the sociological organization of our life together. If we are to adopt a more fluid structure for the Christian community this must be deeply rooted in our understanding of God. . . . In recent years there has been a renewed interest in the doctrine of God; in particular there has been a growing realization that the life of the people of God is intimately connected to the being of God. God as Father, Son, and Holy Spirit in relationship, Trinity in unity, has been understood as the defining pattern for the church.[20]

Ward's proposal moves beyond the Trinity as a profound theological concept. The Trinity is the source and pattern for networked Christian communities and all human relationality. A robust doctrine of God is the theological heart of the central control box in emerging church communities. God is experienced as radical transcendence and radical immanence. All three members of the Trinity are given equal importance in worship. A deeply trinitarian understanding of God serves as the basis for the valuing of relationship and community. Classical Lutheran sensibilities about the priesthood of all believers and Christian vocation inform and express such a trinitarian understanding of Christian life and practice.

17. Ancient-future orthodoxy

The ancient-future orientation is a strong impulse in many emerging church communities. An ancient-future connection between pre-modern texts and traditions and postmodern life and curiosities may be sensed and explored. Preaching, teaching, and the texts of songs, hymns, and rituals are classically orthodox in substance. However, we must remember that these churches seek an authentic experience of God within community. Classically orthodox texts from the storehouse of the great Christian tradition must be culturally authenticated in particular communities. "Ancient-Future worship is rooted in Scripture, draws from the great traditions of historic worship, and seeks to be authentic in a post-Christian culture."[21] Among other things, ancient-future means this: being radical in the postmodern era means not tearing up the roots, but going to one's roots to uncover wisdom, direction, and energy.

18. Dialog is valued

The path to understanding is paved by dialog. Emerging church communities have invested in what is perhaps the operative premise of German philosopher Hans Georg-Gadamer: genuine understanding proceeds through dialog or conversation.[22] There is no felt need to judge or condemn other faith traditions or religious expressions. A more fruitful option is to join in conversation with those from other perspectives (religious or otherwise) in order to listen, learn, and broaden one's horizon. Elsewhere I have called this practice evangelical listening, which I believe lies at the heart of cultivating Christ-centered, mutually respectful relationships. The essential premise seems to be engage and be engaged by the "other" and become more fully and truly who you are in the process. Conversation is a figural practice within the life of a community, as well. Many congregations allow time and space for communal midrash after the reading of biblical texts or preaching. Leadership invites questions and comments in response to the texts or proclamation and facilitates public, communal conversation and interpretation.

19. Experience and ritual moments

There is a rich strand of the biblical tradition (most notably in the Acts of the Apostles) and early Christian theological tradition that refers to Christianity as "the Way." The Christian faith is a way of life to be embodied, a way of being human in the world to which one aspires. Emerging church communities strive to create a deeply participatory environment that fosters full, active, and conscious participation in a complete spiritual and physical sense. Real, actual experience—of the individual or the group—is always paramount. For instance, corporate worship often includes "ritual moments," opportunities for personal, spiritual connection in the midst of the gathered community. Various practices are employed for such ritual moments, including silence, silent and guided meditation, various expressions and postures of prayer (for example, prayer labyrinth), full and ample use of the arts, and the creation of indigenous music, to name a few.

20. Honoring the question(s)

Emerging church communities value the power of the question. Probing questions are honored and expected, which makes leadership neither reactive nor defensive. In fact, leaders appreciate genuine inquiry and seek to cultivate an environment that is open to such inquiry. In light of this commitment to valuing questions and inquiry, a popular misconception is that emerging church communities have little regard for answers or a notion of "truth." Critics of the emerging church conversation have had a field day leveling this criticism, often under the guise of some form of relativism. To the contrary, emerging church communities as Christian communities embody deep belief, often using the historic creeds of the great Christian tradition as the primary gauge. However, there is a strong sense that in order to effectively communicate with others, one must know what the questions are—whether implicit or explicit to a person's life circumstance and spiritual questing.

To honor the question is to honor the one who asks; honoring the other creates the fertile soil for trust. Trust is the necessary foundation for authentic relationships; authentic relationships are the bedrock of communal formation.

21. Being in the neighborhood

At one level, emerging church communities see themselves as one neighbor among many others in a particular local setting. There is a strong desire to cultivate relationships and develop partnerships with other people, institutions, and organizations in order to work together for the health and well-being of the neighborhood. Interestingly, the heavy accent on being church by investing in the neighborhood is seldom (if ever) a front for what the modern church has called "evangelism." Indeed, focused attention to the people and places where one lives might lead, on occasion, to opportunities for Christian witness. Mostly such attention and investment affords the opportunity to practice neighbor love and serve others. A "neighbor-as-servant" orientation seeks to practice the presence of Christ in a particular locale, among and alongside the various neighbors present in that setting. Being church means being rooted in the particularity of a given context, giving oneself away in love and service to the other.

22. Radically indigenous

Emerging church communities have been described as "radically indigenous." They are not to be confused with popular modernist models such as the mega-church or contemporary worship or the church growth approach. In many ways, the emerging church is the coming-of-age of "Gen X" and "Gen Y" sensibilities, though emerging church communities are not at all to be understood in abstract generational or conceptual categories. They are deliberately adapting their understanding and practice of church to fit their cultural and local environments driven by a figural question: "What does it mean to be who we are where we are?" This is anything but a one-time question. It is a life-orienting question that is continually asked and to which the community continually seeks to discern a response.

Questions for Reflection & Discussion

1. How do you understand the "cultural sea change" described in the first part of this chapter? How have you experienced the significant changes and transition that was discussed?

2. What did you know about the emerging church conversation before reading this chapter? What do you think about it now?

3. What does it mean for the church to be church today? What does it mean for your church community to be church where you are?

4. Twenty-two common principles and practices shared by a wide variety of emerging church communities were discussed in this chapter. Which do you find most interesting and potentially fruitful for ministry? Most challenging? Where do you see resonance with what is happening in your church community?

5

Mobile Leadership: Navigating New Wilderness Roads

I recently searched for the word "leadership" on the Internet and received 170 million hits. Narrowing the field to church leadership resulted in more than 7.5 million hits. I think it's safe to say that whether in the corporation or the congregation, leadership is a hot issue. Both large corporations and large congregations alike devote staff and seminars to leadership development. Many major universities now have formed leadership institutes. Everybody seems interested.

While history and human affairs arguably have always been intrigued with and influenced by leaders, there seems to be a reemergence of keen interest in leadership—in the North American context, in the life of the church, in the whole world over—perhaps precipitated by the massive and sudden changes that have taken place these past few decades. It's not that change is unique to this time in history, that we somehow have a monopoly on change. There has always been change; some would say that the only thing you can count on is change. The point that I want to make—and it's not like this is some original insight of mine—is that change has changed.

Somewhere in the mid-twentieth century the nature of change itself changed. Change became random and episodic, often happening in quantum leaps. One of the primary symbols of the larger culture in which we now live is the microchip processor. We live in a world of "raplexity"—a combination of speed and complexity. In this kind of an environment, we have learned that one can hardly survive, let alone thrive, simply by working harder and harder. Doing things the "old way" only faster and continually seeking to improve communication are dead-ends. Discontinuous change has had a particularly disastrous impact on established church leaders and institutions. Bill Easum contends that "nothing in our past has prepared us for ministry in today's world."[1] Leonard Sweet suggests that those born after 1965 are the first generation in history that does not need authority figures to access information:

> They don't need representative authority figures to get information. This new world gets information a thousand different ways. They want to know something more from their mentors than, "I have to come to you to get information." They want to know how to perform that information, how to model it, in short they want to be "mentored" in using that information. The whole culture and the underpinnings of culture have shifted from a print culture whose emphasis was on representation to an electronic and soon bionomic culture whose emphasis is on participation.[2]

Within the life of the churches in a post-whatever era, futurists are calling for a focus on and reevaluation of the concept of leadership within the Christian communities. This is also a day in which the church is seeking to rediscover and redefine its mission. It is clear to many that a new twenty-first century church is emerging, and among its chief characteristics are both a clarified focus on its mission and a clear understanding of the cultural context in which it does its mission. Yea, so many years ago, Loren Mead was a harbinger of this now widely-accepted insight. His thesis is that a new church is being born around us, and three things are happening simultaneously:

First, our present confusion about mission hides the fact that we are facing a fundamental change in how we understand the mission of the church. Beneath the confusion we are being stretched between a great vision of the past and a new vision that is not fully formed. Second, local congregations are now being challenged to move from a passive, responding role in support of mission to a front-line, active role. The familiar roles of laity, clergy, executive, bishop, church council, and denominational bureaucrat are in profound transition all around us. Third, institutional structures and forms developed to support one vision of our mission are rapidly collapsing. I argue that we are being called to invent or reinvent structure and forms that will serve the new mission. . . . I believe that we are being called to be midwives for a new church.[3]

Carl George casts his vote for decentralized leadership, a bottom-up vision of ministry wherein, "The church leader of the future will look more like a music director than a bureaucratic leader."[4] Leonard Sweet speaks of a church with only two categories of leadership—"baptized ministers" and "ordained ministers," and even goes so far as to suggest that anyone truly interested in doing ministry shouldn't get ordained. We are, particularly in the churches, standing at the precipice—or perhaps in the midst of—a crisis in leadership.

In such a fluid socio-cultural situation, Pete Ward imagines a church that is more liquid as it lives. I'm intrigued by Ward's proposal, intrigued enough to tinker around with a notion of leadership—fluid cultures, liquid church, mobile leadership? Who's to say? Let's tinker with it a bit and see what happens.

Theories of Leadership

There are a variety of ways in which one can think about and imagine leadership. In the literature, one can trace the evolution of thinking about leadership along four basic contours, represented by at least four primary theories regarding leadership and leaders.[5]

1. Arguably the first theory of leadership and the one that continues to be deeply entrenched in the predominant American culture is the "great man" theory. This theory grew out of the nineteenth-century notion that history is the story of great men (sadly, women were not even considered candidates for greatness!) and their impact on the world around them. Trait theorists examine the personality characteristics of the "great ones," and locate their influence and rise to power in a heroic set of personal talents, skills, or physical characteristics.

2. In reaction to the "great man" theory, the situationalists argue that history is much greater than the effects of these persons on the world around them. In other words, the times produce the person and not vice-versa. Situationalists are interested in leaders because of the critical moment at which they lived—a time when a combination of powerful social, political, economic, and religious forces came together. Instead of focusing on a common set of traits, situationalists pay attention to the critical time in history at which various people are called forth to lead (for example, Abraham Lincoln).

3. Transactional theory suggests that one earns the capacity to lead, often by handling the little things well. The focus is on the transactions or interactions by which individuals gain influence and sustain it over time. Leaders not only influence followers but are under their influence as well and earn influence by adjusting to the expectations of followers. In common parlance, if no one is following, then you are not leading. This remains a predominant approach to leadership in the modern corporate setting.

4. Eldership is a fourth theory of leadership. Simply put, one lives long enough to lead. In many cultures (sadly enough, and for the most part, not the predominant American culture) one gains wisdom through life experience, becomes an elder, and thus de facto leads.

The Jonah Narrative as a Biblical Warrant for Leadership

I want to try my hand at another way of thinking about, imagining, and exercising missional, communal leadership. But before we do that, let's visit a kindred spirit from the biblical narrative—someone who was quite familiar with life in, shall we say, a liquid environment. Although perhaps not properly a "theory of leadership" in the more contemporary sense, the historical narrative about the prophet Jonah opens a perspective that I believe fits with what I am trying to say here about Christian communities and leadership.

Many of us know the somewhat comical story of Jonah only too well. Jonah is called by God to deliver a prophetic message to the people of Nineveh. However, it was difficult for Jonah to imagine preaching to that great Assyrian city. Nineveh's great sin was that they had flaunted their enormous power before God and the world through numerous acts of heartless cruelty. Jonah, we learn, is a reluctant prophet; he found his mission distasteful. In response to God's call, Jonah decides to run away from, rather than obey, God. God judges Jonah's disobedience. The result is the strange story of Jonah ending up in the belly of a big fish. After much soul searching and some nudging from God, Jonah repents. God issues the call a second time, and Jonah is obedient. He responds by proclaiming God's prophetic word to the people of Nineveh. The message is terse, simple in content, and difficult to pronounce, let alone hear: "Forty days more, and Nineveh shall be overthrown!" (Jonah 3:4). The result, to Jonah's surprise, is that the people of Nineveh hear, believe, and repent. God decides not to destroy the city, and so on and so forth.

What captures my imagination and invites me to take seriously the Jonah narrative as an analogy for leadership are not some of the usual suspects—Jonah the reluctant, recalcitrant prophet or the fact that God's mind was changed. Rather, it is the manner in and through which leadership was exercised. Look at the third chapter of the book of Jonah. Jonah proclaimed God's word. The people of Nineveh believed God, and in turn they made a proclamation to which the king listened and responded. In other words, the *people led* and the "leader" followed, all in response to the opening created by the public leadership of God through God's word. It is, I believe, an analogy for the kind of leadership needed in Christian communities today in our emerging post-whatever context.

Leadership as Evangelical and Public, Missional and Communal

The church today needs leadership that is evangelical and public, missional and communal. Leadership must emerge out of the particular community in which it is exercised and support the work of God to which the people of God are called in that place. One of the lessons we learn from the Jonah story, translated for this new day, is that leadership is more than "the leader"—whether that be pastor, president, or CEO. Leadership must be broad and shared, as in that old Reformation principle of the priesthood of all believers, and it must be mobile, agile, and ready to engage wherever, whenever. I believe deeply that all of God's gifted people—all of you who are reading these words—are called to leadership in some way.

My imagination for leadership is based on a set of principles and practices—core commitments and beliefs that inform who we are and guide what we do. Here they are; you could probably add your own. In fact, I hope you do. And if you do, please share them with me.

Gospel<>Culture

The Christian gospel and culture(s) cannot be separated, although they are deeply distinguishable. As theologians, leaders are called into this "hinge place" between gospel wisdom and cultural wisdom. Life here can be a bit dicey, characterized by creative tension and involving the hard work of deeply distinguishing the gospel in light of culture and the cultures in light of the Christian gospel. As leaders we must risk living in this tension and resist the notion that somehow people of faith have to choose one or the other—gospel or culture—as if they are opposites or somehow "the culture" is a menace to the gospel. Cultural beliefs or values can be a threat to the wisdom of the Christian gospel in the same way that the "truth" of the gospel, when wielded without regard to the integrity of culture, can be a threat to people. Faithful leaders are called to help these two realties—Christian gospel and cultures—talk to one another and better understand one another. This happens best when the people in a community engage in regular conversation that is open, honest, and, when necessary, critical. Perhaps at one level the task of leadership is to host and facilitate ongoing conversation where interpretation can take place. So, when something like *The Da Vinci Code* makes a big splash in the popular culture pond, the community can discuss and interpret it theologically.

Story<>Mission

We join the work of theology as a servant of God's story, the story of the triune God of the Hebrew and Christian Scriptures. This story that we are called to tend and serve is the story of a God who is mission; mission belongs to God, and God is a God who is for people and for the world. In other words, central to the story of the triune God is the *missio Dei* (the mission of God). The Christian faith is intrinsically missionary and reflects the dynamic relationship between God and the world, the ultimate expression of which is Jesus Christ. God continues to communicate the good news that became incarnate in Jesus—that God is a God-for-people and for the world—through the *viva vox evangellii,* the living voice of the gospel. The living Word of God is a word that is read, preached, and heard, and a word that is visible and lived.

Christians are storied people, but for Christ followers this story is not about us, but a story about God into which we have been invited as a gift. It is this story that defines who we are and shapes how we are to be in the world as human beings. Servant leaders know the importance of trusting the promise, and they are grounded and rooted in the triune God as persons of faith. God's people are storied people, "steeped in the lore" of the Christian tradition—dwelling in the story, listening to the story, speaking the story as a living Word, and seeking to live the story.

Mission<>Vision

Who hasn't read or heard, in recent years, about the need to have a vision? A growing number of churches have joined the trend, longstanding in the corporate world, of crafting vision statements, mission statements, value statements, or outcome statements.

I'm not necessarily anti-statement, but from a theological perspective the order does matter: vision follows mission. Leaders are called to have a sense of vision, both personally and corporately, but mission (as I am interpreting it) comes first. Mission belongs to God—the God who is for people and for the world—and is intrinsic to the Christian faith. Vision is a particular, contextual response to God's mission—in churches, in communities, and in the world. In short, vision is the discerning of mission in context.

Indigenous, missionary Christian communities join God in God's work in the world in particular times, in particular places, and with particular people. I realize that I am using the word *particular* a lot, but it's important that we descend into detail and understand as best we can what is distinctive about the moment in history during which we are alive and the specific place where that history is unfolding. The Christian faith is lived in community as a response to the God who is in mission—present and active—in the world. Every community of faithful people lives in a context, and that context, in large part, determines the particular ways in which the community joins in ministry together. The question that vision asks is this: What does it mean to be who we are where we are? In other words, what is God up to here?

One of the critical tasks of leadership is to serve as theological interlocutor and guide—convening, hosting, participating in, and helping to sustain a conversation—as the community discerns and seeks to live its vision for mission. What languages, methods, and resources are needed by leadership and a particular community of faith to carry out faithful, truthful, and effective ministry for the sake of God's mission? This is the hard work that must be taken up by each and every community of God's people—discerning the very specific, concrete ways in which God's story might be heard, believed, and lived in a particular context.

Characteristics of Effective Leadership

If the core commitments I have named are the moorings for the kind of leadership I imagine—evangelical and public, missional and communal—then the following characteristics give expression to such leadership. In the sections that follow I wish to consider a constellation of characteristics: modeling and mentoring, self-definition or differentiated leadership, the public character of theological leadership, unleashing giftedness, and collaboration and the use of power.

Modeling<>Mentoring

Although faithful modeling and effective mentoring are marks of leadership, this first characteristic is also a hinge, the point of transition between the commitments already identified and further marks of leadership yet to be explored. When it comes to leadership formation, people need more than a good role model; people need to be apprenticed or mentored. The combination of mentoring and leadership development equals apprenticeship, which seems to be a lost art these days. Case in point: consider the relationship between Moses and Joshua, narrated here and there in Exodus, Numbers, Joshua, and Judges. Though the biblical narrative is rife with examples of mentoring relationships, the relationship between Moses and Joshua exemplifies the significance of grooming the person or people who will join you, follow you, or even replace you.

The time has long passed when one needs authority figures or authorized structures to access information. So many people today have quick access to a staggering amount of information. The combination of unbridled access to information and diffuse boundaries available from today's technology creates a tempting and potentially toxic environment in which to live, particularly for our children and young people—anything is available in cyberspace, just search it. MySpace, FaceBook, private chat rooms, weblogs—it's a big world getting closer and moving faster all the time.

Leaders are needed who have the capacity to model and mentor the using of information in a society that is increasingly on information overload. What many people today desperately need—especially the youngest in our midst—are those who are wiser, more seasoned, who can demonstrate how one "performs" information, that is, how to critically interpret information and use it in ways that are life-giving, appropriate, safe, responsible, not to mention faithful and truthful. In short, we need people as well as institutions who can use information in such a way that it contributes to the common good in a civil society.

So, the very practice of modeling and mentoring or apprenticing others is a critical leadership characteristic in and of itself. It is not accidental; it is an intentional practice, most often instigated by the one doing the mentoring, that takes time and commitment.

Although there are many other leadership capacities that need to be taught and modeled throughout the people of God, I have chosen four that are critical for the formation and diffusion of leadership in Christian communities today.

Differentiation<>Self-Definition

Seminary students are used to writing papers. The garden-variety, twelve- to fifteen-page paper is (sadly) the default in much of academia for evaluating students. As a teacher, however, I've come to a startling realization in my small experience as a seminary professor: If students write papers, then someone—namely, me as the professor—has to read them. As a rule, students don't like to write them and I don't like to read them. So, I try to come up with alternative methods for evaluating students that fit with the purpose and content of a particular course or assignment. I'm not against writing; I'm just for variety and creativity in pedagogy.

The one exception to the I'll-do-anything-to-avoid-writing-a-paper-mantra I've heard from students comes annually in the class I teach on leadership. Students would do almost anything to avoid what many say is the most difficult and uncomfortable assignment they have ever been given: Find someone you trust, a person who knows you, really knows you, and ask them to answer these questions honestly: Who do people say that I am? How do you perceive me? How do others perceive me? When was the last time you asked someone that question? Like many of my students, most of us (myself included) naturally want to avoid this like the plague.

But as you well know, our life in Christian community is filled with occasions—planned and unplanned, structured and unstructured—when we function in and as "small groups." Sure, we dress them up with other names—the congregational council, the parish vestry, the education task force, or the dreaded property committee. Regardless, they are all small groups. In many ways that is how human beings function in community—in groups. It is most certainly the way that our life together in churches is structured.

We are all a part of those groups, sometimes as the designated leader and at other times not. Regardless of how we are a part, we are a part and we participate. The question becomes: How are we a part? How do we function in the midst of others? How are we perceived by others? Whether we like it or not, we are perceived by others based in large part on how we interact with other people. We each have the capacity to be the kind of person who either invites others in or alienates them. In other words, we can be an alienating presence or an inviting presence. And it's never cut-and-dried. We can all be both, from time to time, to varying degrees. Perhaps that is one of the many reasons that the Christian (and especially Lutheran) tradition has come to see human beings as *simul justus et peccatur*—at the same time saint and sinner. It works for me.

That's also why leaders need the self-critical capacity to think about how we interact with others and to check in with others about this. We can all be masters of self-deception and cannot simply trust our own self-critical capacity, no matter how well-honed that capacity might be. This is why I have my students participate in an exercise that most of us despise. I want this "academic exercise" to become a regular practice in ministry, an example of asking difficult questions, listening to honest responses, and continuing to grow as a leader. In technical jargon, this has to do with a concept called differentiation.

Leadership understands and practices the concept of differentiation as people living and leading in systems. For our purposes here, those systems are Christian communities, often called congregations. Leaders in such systems are not only self-defined but also "God-defined" as people of faith. In fact, from a biblical and theological perspective, a person's self-definition grows out of her or his identity as a forgiven sinner and baptized child of God. Practicing differentiation as a leader means the ability to be an "I" in the midst of others; to be an "I" and stay connected in and to a community of people.

If you believe, as I suggested earlier, that every Christian community is called to the continual work of discerning a vision, then someone has to make sure that this work of discernment gets done. Leaders are those who "steward the vision" of the community. Vision is a community's way of defining itself in mission and charting a course with God toward the future. Systemic thinkers like Edwin Friedman suggest that a vision must be forged and articulated by leaders who are themselves well-differentiated persons. In other words, being a "steward of the vision" entails being a "steward of the self." Being a "steward of the self" means defining oneself, regulating one's own anxiety, staying connected to others, encouraging the gifts and resources of others, and staying the course, that is, sticking to the vision when things get messy or bumpy.

I was critical earlier in this book about how family systems theory—and the work of Ed Friedman in particular—has led to the popularity of church-as-family thinking among many people. There are, nonetheless, some valuable insights in Friedman's work for an understanding of leadership. Edwin Friedman was a student of Murray Bowen and worked from within the Bowenian multigenerational school of family systems theory (how's that for a mouthful). Although much of Friedman's work focused on the three "families" of clergy (the personal family of clergy, the congregational family itself, and the families within the congregation), I am interested in an understanding of leadership that moves beyond clergy only. Friedman identifies five basic, interrelated concepts that distinguish the family model from the individual model. One of the primary concepts with which he works is *differentiation of self.*

Differentiation of self is the capacity of a person to define one's own life goals and values apart from the surrounding togetherness pressures of others; to say "I" when others are demanding "you" and "we." The well-differentiated person has developed a core self that generates her or his own thinking, feeling, decisions, and actions, which fosters the development of mutually respectful, satisfying, and supportive relationships with others. Differentiation also entails the ability to maintain a non-anxious presence in the midst of anxiety and to take responsibility for one's own destiny and emotional being. For instance, in a situation of conflict, there are a number of ways that a person can respond: to fuse (emotionally enmesh), to distance (run away), or to self-define. The task of differentiation is the capacity to be an "I" while remaining connected to others. One key to faithful and effective leadership—articulating and seeking a vision in response to God's mission and tending to the health and well-being of the community and its leadership—has more to do with the capacity of leaders to self-define than with their ability to motivate or persuade others.

Leadership through self-definition is more a way of thinking and being than a set of techniques. The basic concept of leadership through self-definition is this: if each person attends primarily to one's own role and responsibilities in the community, in concert with the vision, while staying in touch (communicating and connecting) with the rest of the community, there is a more than reasonable chance that the community will move together in mission toward the vision that has been discerned. Leaders aspire to an emotionally healthy lifestyle: open and honest communication, participating in the ongoing conversation of the community, self-defined yet connected to others in safe, respectful, and appropriate relationships.

Any Christian community is much bigger than "family," and leadership is exercised by more than the clergy or rostered leaders. The community of faith is called to be a mission outpost, a gospel community that gives itself away in ministry and service to God's world. Pastoral leadership is bigger than the pastor or any professional leader. Pastoral leadership belongs to the entire community as the body of Christ. Leadership is well-served when the focus becomes coaching, equipping, empowering, and mobilizing people of all ages to discern and share their God-given gifts in ministry, in harmony with a vision for the sake of God's mission.

Theological Conversation<>Public

In Christian communities, those who lead are called to be proactive in encouraging civil, reciprocal, public conversation about issues that matter, and model the use of healthy, mature faith language. There is an openness and willingness to engage publicly the issues of God's world on behalf of God, and a conviction that the Christian community is a key context for this kind of deliberation and dialog.

Perhaps more than anything, this leadership commitment or characteristic has to do with the texture of "the church" as a very broad and diverse constellation of Christian communities. So often reference is made to "the church." What is "the church"? What is it about? What is it for? From the perspective of my own tradition represented in the Evangelical Lutheran Church in America, this question is often answered by referring to the Article VII of the Augsburg Confession, which states:

> It is also taught among us that one holy Christian church will be and remain forever. This is the assembly of believers among whom the Gospel is preached in its purity and the holy sacraments are administered according to the Gospel.[6]

A classical and widely-accepted interpretation of what this means is that the church is fundamentally an event—the "happening" of the gospel. This has become an almost default interpretation for Lutherans, and I fear it often has caused us to fixate a bit too much on church or congregation as place.

Professor Cheryl Peterson suggests that the Evangelical Lutheran Church in America does not yet have an agreed-upon ecclesiology.[7] This lack of an agreed-upon ecclesiology has led to a number of difficulties for the ELCA, most significantly, the challenge of mission today.

> So where might Lutherans turn in order to reclaim a theological understanding of the nature and mission of the church for the challenges of our context today, especially that of mission? There seem to be two main approaches and an emerging third. . . . 1) reclaim the Reformers' view of the church as given in the Lutheran Confessional writings, especially Articles 7 & 8 of the Augsburg Confession (1530) as sufficient for a contemporary Lutheran ecclesiology; 2) recover the ecclesiology of the "Great Tradition," classical Christianity interpreted and practiced in accord with the traditions of the early church; or 3) develop a "missional ecclesiology" from a Trinitarian understanding of *missio Dei*.[8]

She prefers door #3, and I think that she is spot on. The task before us is to expose and respond to the missional challenges and opportunities that we face today.

What does it mean to be who we are where we are? Being church today means living God's mission where we are. To paraphrase the language of Scripture, the church exists in the world, is not of the world, and yet is decidedly for the world. It is for the world because this is God's world that we inhabit. The triune God of the Christian faith is a God-for-the-world and a God-for-people. Could it be that what happens *through* the assembly of believers is just as important as what happens in the assembly of believers? We need church communities today that are rooted deeply in God's Word of promise through Christ and yet are more nimble, agile, and mobile in how they practice the art of evangelical listening and living.

The people of God have been entrusted with the gospel, the good news of God's Christ as the promise of salvation for the whole creation. Being a steward of this mystery is a great privilege that entails even greater responsibility. The Christian gospel is grounded in the event of Jesus. This grounding is the basis for our confession of God as well as for the experience of the Christian community. And the proclamation of God's good news is always directed—it is good news to or good news for an "other" or others. Jesus Christ is the norm for how the mission of the Christian gospel is carried out and embodied in God's world. "The church" is a very broad and diverse collection of people who aspire to proclaim and live the gospel in and through community for God's world. In this way, the mission of "the church" is to gospel God's world, that is, to proclaim and seek to embody the Word and the Way of the triune God who is for, with, and in God's world.

One of the vocations (callings) of a Christian community is to be the kind of place where people can hash things out. In order to do that, the people who comprise the community need to be the kind of people who are willing to hash things out together. One of my former teachers, Professor Gary Simpson, who teaches theology at Luther Seminary in St. Paul, was fond of saying that while most of us can *argue in public*, few of us have the ability to *argue publicly*. What he's getting at, among other things, is the need today for people who are capable of engaging in civil, public conversations that are forthright and honest without becoming mean-spirited. The world in which we live, the society of which we are a part, desperately needs places where such discussions can take place. Christian communities are called to be those kinds of places. Christian communities that are called, gathered, enlightened, and sanctified by the Holy Spirit are public meeting spaces to which all people are invited and in which all of the world's business can be discussed and deliberated. Christian communities that are fashioned in the way of Jesus have a kiosk-at-the-farmers-market mentality. They set up shop to talk more than trade; to make friends, not money. The world needs Christian communities that do a better job of living in the spirit of Jesus. Face it, many of the people who do not come to a church, who are not connected to a Christian community, care less initially about what Christians believe and pay much more attention to how Christians behave. I'm no moral crusader, but maybe it's time that Christians started acting more Christ-like.

Giftedness<>Discernment

Clericalism—the class distinction between clergy and laity (that is, the professional and the amateur), is "...one of the most insidious distinctions ever developed by the church."[9] According to Leonard Sweet, we live in an age when there is no longer a culturally assumed and approved benefit of clergy.

> The church is ruled by a clerical minority that carries on about institutional matters of deep interest to the clerical minority (ordination issues, language of the liturgy, etc.) rather than the true concerns of most church members. . . . The clerical era of the church is apparently nearing an end as the people of God reject the class separation. Many church members think it is time to deemphasize clergy as well as "dechurch." The driving force of the church must be the "laity," not the "clergy." The pastoral leadership of baptized ministers is missing in the oldline church today.[10]

It should be said that this critique of clericalism is not simply one of the latest fads being wordsmithed by a theological futurist such as Sweet. Well over twenty years ago Joseph Sittler, whom Martin Marty refers to as our sage and our seer, shared a similar concern in responding to a question about the uniqueness of the ordained ministry. According to Sittler, "the church insists on preparing a designated cadre to see to it that the constitutive story is told, and that the nurturing sacraments are administered. . . . This is a way of defining the ordained pastorate of the church that does not elevate it above the laity, but gives it a particular job among the people of God."[11] The bottom line is the same: Equating "real ministry" with the ordained deprives the whole people of God of their ability to conduct ministry and exercise the priesthood of all believers.

One of my favorite *Far Side* cartoons shows a young boy, book under his arm, pushing on a door that says "Pull." The caption reads, "Midvale School for the Gifted." Too many of our churches spend way too much creative time and energy going *in* the *out* door, trying to get people in, whence in reality we need to work on getting more people out. Our churches are full of tremendously gifted, passionate people. Leadership that is committed to an ongoing process of helping people to discern, discover, claim, and share their God-given gifts will unleash the gifts of the Spirit and the giftedness of the people of God. Leaders multiply leaders by apprenticing and coaching others in discovering, identifying, affirming, and using the gifts that God has given them, thereby equipping and empowering more and more people to use their gifts "for the work of ministry, for building up the body of Christ" (Eph. 4:12).

A focus on spiritual gifts, the giftedness of the congregation, and unleashing these gifts in and through the community represents a faithful and effective method for remediating the issue of clericalism. Christian communities are called to be holy places, open spaces where people can discover and share their unique set of gifts and talents—guided by a communal vision for mission and energized by the Holy Spirit. A focus on giftedness allows the community to build on the creativity and strengths of the people rather than their weaknesses, which is often cast in the language of "need." It fosters a spirit of mutual accountability and creative expectation (a necessary ingredient in a teaming culture, as we shall soon see) within a community

The first Reformation returned the word of God to the people of God. A second reformation, underway at this present moment, is seeking to return the work of God to the people of God as more and more people come to understand and act on the belief that they are called, gifted, and empowered as ministers of the gospel. Trying to go *in* the *out* door translates into, "How can we employ more laity as church workers?" There is a dicey, seemingly innocuous but potentially dangerous assumption here—that all viable ministry happens inside the church walls. The better question, I think, amounts to sending people *out* the *out* door: "How can the people of God—gifts in one hand, creativity in the other—be sent by God as apostles to impact God's world for Christ?" The challenge before us is to send God's gifted people *out* the *out* door and see their primary ministry assignment as being good news wherever God places them: homes, schools, workplaces, communities, marketplaces, civic clubs, even a kiosk at the farmers market. Unleashing the giftedness of the people of God is a key to being church today, living God's mission, and exercising mobile leadership in the spirit of Jesus.

Power<>Collaboration

One of my all-time favorite pieces of dialog from a film takes place in *The Matrix Reloaded,* of the Matrix trilogy fame. Neo is talking with the Oracle and asks about another character (Merovingian), "What does he want?" The Oracle replies, "What do all men (sic) with power want? More power."[12] People gain power and wield power in a variety of ways. One might possess great charisma while another employs brute strength, and yet another uses the power of persuasion. Regardless, all are powerful and can influence others, for better or for worse, by brandishing power. Power dynamics exist, to some degree or another, in all human relationships and within all human communities. We live in a world where power is a reality and a consistent topic of conversation—a reality and conversation to which churches are not immune.

Christian communities are places where power is brokered in many and various ways by a wide variety of people, often in some type of relationship to authority roles and structures. In fact, in the life of a church (particularly those that are part of a large denomination), there is more often than not a complex relationship between power, authority, and leadership.[13] Yet the reality of the power that circulates in and through the people in a community is dwarfed by the ultimate power present and active in and through the triune God. A critical task of leadership is to keep the community aware of how power is circulating in a given place and open to the Holy Spirit, revealing where the life of the community must change in order to conform to the gospel.

Creating a communal ethos characterized by self-awareness and openness is no easy task, but it is possible—and leadership must set the tone. It begins with the historic Christian faith (as articulated by one of the great creeds, for instance, the Apostles' or Nicene) as the lodestar and the communal vision for mission as the banner held high for all to see. Leaders model emotional health and self-definition, choose to risk sharing power, and cultivate the spiritual gifts of the people in the community. Indeed, missional Christian leaders are realistic about the possibilities and limitations involved in using and sharing power, but ultimately they believe in a benevolent dimension of power. Leaders who are committed to collegiality and honest, direct communication and collaborating with others in ministry—simply put, the willingness to invite others in and work together—set the tone for a teaming culture in a community.

This is all to say that leaders must understand the profound importance of exposing and discussing the power dynamics in each and every particular community. This calls for intentionality and careful boldness on the part of leadership to be willing to name the unhealthy use (or abuse) or power when necessary and bring this into the public conversation of the community.

I've hinted at collaboration as a key to living and leading with others in a community, and now I want to lift it up rather blatantly. Collaboration amounts to the many and various members and parts of a community working together—listening, talking, and teaming in order to discern and implement a vision for mission. At its best a community is not afraid to exercise a missional imagination in seeking to work together to discern a vision for mission. This is more like brain-sailing than brainstorming, and generally a lot more enjoyable as well. I like to think of brainstorming as thinking more, which is what most committees tend to do. When confronted with a problem or challenge, the age-old, tried-and-true church basement approach is to form a committee, have meetings, and try to figure out what to do. In sum: think more, solve problem. Brain-sailing involves people who get together, but that is where the similarities end. Brain-sailing is more imaginative, more playful, and is about thinking differently rather than thinking more. "As the Christian community here at St. John's by the gas station in Four Corners, U.S.A., if we could do anything—anything at all—as long as it is in alignment with our vision for mission, what would we do?" Now that's a question that can stir the imagination and get a group of people jazzed for ministry.

A teaming approach to communal leadership is a particular practice of collaboration rooted in the ethos and culture of a community. A teaming culture is an organization or a community whose basic work unit is teams of persons who share a common vision for mission, operate with mutual trust within a web of accountability, and focus on cultivating the gifts of the people in the community. Spiritually grounded, emotionally healthy leaders set the tone for the creation of a teaming culture and invest in an intentional process to foster the elements listed below.

There are at least five elements that characterize a teaming culture. Although seemingly obvious, the *first* element needs to be stated emphatically: in a teaming culture, people work together in teams and not as individuals. Because this is a new approach to work for many people, it requires both a new mindset and more often than not new structures. *Secondly,* a teaming culture possesses a shared, communally discerned vision for mission that defines the boundaries and drives the community forward in ministry. A fundamental premise of living and leading from within a teaming culture is that nothing happens if it does not fit with the vision for mission. The *next mark* of a teaming culture is trust; teaming cultures cannot exist without trust. A sense of deep trust woven into the fabric of a teaming culture builds a web of accountability. In a teaming culture, persons are accountable first to the vision for mission, which means that the standard is the same for everyone involved. The *fourth* element of a teaming culture is a focus on giftedness (to which ample time has been devoted already in the previous section of this proposal). *Finally,* a teaming culture cultivates systems thinking wherein the communal focus is both expanded and opened. The focus is expanded to include the whole of the community and its surrounding environs and opened to discern continually the presence and activity of God as the primary agent in the life and ministry of the community.

The approach to leadership that is being cultivated here—leadership that is evangelical and public, missional and communal—suggests, perhaps more than anything else, that the context of leadership has changed because of the complex and pervasive effect of the changing nature of change itself. The culture of what is broadly understood as American society, as well as the many and various cultures that comprise it, has changed. The nature and shape of organizations have changed. Structures are becoming less and less hierarchical, mechanical, and institutional and more and more decentralized, organic, and fluid in organizing to accomplish their mission. Therefore, the role of the leader has changed, is changing, and must continue to adapt to ever-changing circumstances today.

The time has passed for leadership to be characterized by a "command and control" approach, the goal of which is to be in charge. The emerging role of leadership is characterized by different dimensions: articulating, communicating, and modeling the mission, vision, commitments, and values of the community; aligning the structure of the community—its staff and systems—with the communities vision for mission; implementing appropriate mechanisms, processes, and methods that will serve and accomplish the particular vision for mission; gift-based identification and development of leaders at all levels of Christian life, practice, and ministry; and, simply put, leading—embracing the change, navigating the transition, and narrating the life of the community.

Leadership for the Churches Today

As one might expect, there are major implications that accompany this change in the context of leadership and role of the leader. The "how" of the leadership that is emerging is based on *being* first, and not *doing*. Churches need leaders who are grounded in the *missio Dei,* guided by the Spirit, and focused on the missional vision and values of the community rather than gaining warrant by virtue of a hierarchical position. Authenticity and integrity in relationships and communication are fundamental requirements. Leadership grows out of the leader's self-critical understanding of her or his Christian identity, gifts, and passion. It is exercised within the context of a leadership team, wherein the individual roles are discerned by one's sense of call to ministry, God-given gifts and points of passion, in harmony with those of the others on the team. In any given community, there is no one "leadership style," only a widely gifted variety of leaders seeking to work in harmony and stoke the fires of the Holy Spirit.

In the final analysis, leadership must always fit the cultural setting in which it exists. Thus, being a leader means being a participant (and not sole creator) in the communal task of discerning a vision for mission in a particular setting. Leaders draw out and articulate the collective vision of a community, and then both serve and protect that vision through an ongoing process of open conversation and Spirit-guided discernment. In this process, leaders ask questions like, "What are the needs, gifts, abilities, and passions in and of this community?" and, "How do we serve the mission of the Christian gospel in this time and place?" What is at stake here is a process, not a product.

Leadership today involves interpreting experiences more than imparting knowledge. The relationship between knowledge and experience has shifted. In the emerging cultures, like it or not, experience precedes and validates knowledge. In what some analysts call an "experience economy," people generally experience something first, and the experience creates the context for learning. No longer are leaders in Christian communities mere ecclesiastical information gurus. More importantly, they are guides and interpreters of the experience of the faithful—experience of which they are also a part. Specifically, leaders do this in the narrative context of God's story and their own particular tradition of interpreting that larger story.

Finally, leadership today means being an apostle who leads the community of faith in openly engaging, critically embracing, and mutually transforming culture(s). The point no longer is to supply religious goods and services. Rather, leadership helps the community critically interpret and understand, connect with, and, guided by the Spirit, join in ministry by befriending the larger community and loving and serving the neighbor. No doubt, leading in this way requires a different set of leadership skills. One must be able to listen deeply and translate in order to help the community of faith discern how it is uniquely able to minister in the surrounding community and culture. One must be able to extract and synthesize, which means discerning the embedded passions, gifts, and abilities of the community and identifying ways in which they can be expressed in concrete, useable forms of ministry. And leaders must be able to tell God's story, which means helping the community see themselves in light of what God has done, is doing, and has promised to do. This is the poetic work of leadership: narrating and re-narrating the life of a community. The experience of the faithful and their stories are interpreted and understood within the context of the overarching story of God's redemptive history.

The approach to leadership that I am cultivating here is shaped by a disposition that is deeply storied by God—evangelical and public, missional and communal. Out of this disposition emerges an approach to leadership that is art as well as activity, theologically astute, emotionally mature, willing to practice the Christian faith in and out of a community. It is value-laden leadership that names and owns a tradition with a core set of beliefs. Leaders, like every other person in a community, actively participate in the corporate conversation and worship of the community. But leaders, perhaps not like all others, are those who are called to keep the light shining on God's mission in and through the community. Leaders are persistent, tuned in to the promptings of God's Spirit, open to the wisdom of others, willing to take risks, listening, obedient, helping the people to chart a way forward into God's future.

Navigating New Wilderness Roads

In the sixth chapter of Acts, the fledgling, early Christian community, driven by acute need, chose Stephen (among others) to serve as what we would today call a deacon (word and service ministry). Remember a while ago when I said that it is impossible to lead without being a target? Well, Stephen obviously led quite effectively, speaking God's word and serving the needs of others, for soon after he was chosen by the disciples, he was falsely accused and martyred—but not before he had his say (virtually the entire seventh chapter of Acts).

Having witnessed this act of public violence, the apostles scattered throughout the countryside in a somewhat natural and understandable response. They were not deterred, however, from their work and continued to proclaim God's word. Among those who went from place to place proclaiming the Messiah was Philip. His first stop was Samaria, where crowds of people, including Simon, a magic-user, listened, were amazed, and believed his message about Jesus and the kingdom of God. When word of what was happening in Samaria made its way back to Jerusalem, reinforcements were sent to join Philip, namely, Peter and John. Soon thereafter, following a scathing rebuke of the previously converted Simon, Peter and John returned to Jerusalem, the central hub of apostolic ministry. Not Philip; he was sent south toward Gaza along a wilderness road. Philip obeyed and had an amazing encounter along the way. His experience with the Ethiopian eunuch is paradigmatic and holds many clues and cues for the kind of ministry to which we are called today.

From all appearances, the Ethiopian eunuch was a powerful man. A court official of the Candace, queen of the Ethiopians, he was in charge of her entire treasury. He rode on a chariot that presumably was escorted by an armed guard. He had been to Jerusalem to worship and was returning home. It is no small distance between Jerusalem and Ethiopia. Like many of us, as he rides, he reads—not *Harry Potter* or Jan Karon or Tom Clancy—but an ancient manuscript of the prophet Isaiah. Apparently it was captivating enough to rouse this man's curiosity and prompt a question or two.

This text is ripe with questions that remain unanswered. Why was this eunuch in Jerusalem in the first place? How did he come to worship while he was there? Did he go there with the express purpose of worshiping, or did he see the flyer posted on a pillar and decide on a whim to check it out? Was this powerful man, so entrusted with responsibility by his queen, denied access to the inner sanctum? Was he, too, relegated to the outer court, along with all of the others—women, lepers, foreigners—who were marginalized by those with the privilege of power and status (men and insiders)? And how in the world did this eunuch get his hands on a manuscript? This was long before Guttenberg and his printing press came along, you know. Did money speak as loudly then as it does now? So many questions and so much about which to wonder.

Oddly enough, Philip doesn't bother himself with any of these questions. He pays attention to the prompts he is given by the Spirit and the eunuch. The Spirit instructs Philip to go to the chariot and "join it." He goes, but he does not "join it," not exactly, whatever joining it might mean. Okay, so maybe Philip doesn't do exactly what the Spirit says—but he does go. One might assume he approaches the chariot carefully, cautiously, taking time to listen before asking a question: "Do you understand what you are reading?" "Not exactly," replies the eunuch, "I need help. I need a guide." Now Philip gets in the chariot—after he is invited. Perhaps there is a lesson here for all of us impatient, over-zealous, door-knocking, tract-passing-out, I-want-to-see-results-right-now evangelists. Perhaps there is also a lesson for all of us way-too-patient, I-don't-know-what-to-say-or-what-do-do, well-intentioned-but-not-always-willing, "Who me?" evangelists. Philip plays the hand he is dealt and responds to the questions he is asked. There is the sense that one earns the right to speak by being patient, being present, and listening one's way into the story of another. There is wisdom in learning what the questions are before one attempts to respond.

Philip modeled this approach. He spoke after he had listened. He began where the eunuch "was at," so to speak, and started with the particular scripture he was given. It reminds me of the phrase used often by the St. Joan of Arc Catholic community in Minneapolis: "Wherever you are on the journey." Philip joined this eunuch where he was at, both literally and figuratively. Dig a pit for the cross, wherever you are, and there you begin. That's exactly what Philip did. In this text, he waited a long time before he "spoke." But when the time was right, he did speak to this man about Jesus the Messiah.

And, lo and behold, on this wilderness road, they came across some water. Now there are a lot of things for which human beings need water, namely, drinking and bathing, both of which would be at the top of my list when on a trip along a wilderness road. Not this eunuch; this man asked to be baptized, which means (obviously) he knew something about baptism. Apparently, there was nothing to prevent a baptism along this wilderness road. They both went into the water and the eunuch was baptized. Immediately after the baptism, Philip was snatched away. Snatched is a cool word, a vibrant, full-of-action word. Philip didn't saunter on down the road, fading away into the sunset; nor was he merely taken, a word that has much more propriety to it. The Spirit snatched him and no one seemed worse for the wear—neither Philip nor the eunuch. In fact, the eunuch left rejoicing, which I take to mean, full of joy. And Philip? Well, Philip found himself elsewhere—in a different place with different people but with same call: live the good news before you speak it.

This was not only Philip's call; it is our call as well. But it is not only our call; it is our story, too. We join those whom we meet along the way, those who are searching and seeking, questing and questioning. We join them, whatever that means, and accompany them "wherever they are on the journey." And as we do, perhaps, just maybe, we too will meet the Christ whom we seek. The dayspring from on high, the bright morning star, the Lamb of God, Jesus, the Christ of God, our journey's end and our final rest.

Questions for Reflection & Discussion

1. One of the only things you can count on is change—do you agree or disagree? How do you deal with change? How has change itself changed?

2. Read the whole book of Jonah from beginning to end. If you are in a group setting, have someone read it aloud so it can be "heard." What captures your imagination as you read and/or hear this text?

3. Which principles and practices—core commitments and beliefs—inform who we are and guide what we do as leaders in Christian communities?

4. It's time to end as we began—by reading the story of Philip and the Ethiopian eunuch in Acts 8:26-40. Where are you in your journey of faith? To what or to whom is the text calling you?

Notes

Preface
1. Rainer Maria Rilke, *Letters to a Young Poet,* rev. ed. (New York: W. W. Norton & Company, 1993), 34–35.

Chapter 1
1. John Dominic Crossan, *The Dark Interval* (Santa Rosa, Calif.: Polebridge Press, 1988), 99–100.
2. Wilhelm Loehe, *Three Books about the Church,* trans. and ed. James L. Schaaf (Philadelphia: Fortress Press, 1969), 59.
3. For an excellent but fairly thick summary of this "cultural sea change" see the Introduction: "Where We Stand" to *The Blackwell Companion to Postmodern Theology* (Oxford: Blackwell Publishers, 2001). University of Manchester theologian Graham Ward, who is also author of the Introduction, edits the book.
4. Stephen Neill, *A History of Christian Missions,* 2nd ed. (London: Penguin Books, 1991), 14–15.
5. David B. Barrett and Todd M. Johnson, "Annual Statistical Table on Global Mission: 1998," *International Bulletin of Missionary Research,* XXII, 1 (January 1998): 26–27.
6. Philip Jenkins, *The Next Christendom: The Coming of Global Christianity* (New York: Oxford University Press, 2002) is a very thorough and credible book that narrates the rise of global Christianity.
7. David Bosch, *Transforming Mission: Paradigm Shifts in Theology of Mission,* American Society of Missiology Series, No. 16 (Maryknoll, N.Y.: Orbis Books, 1991), 390.
8. Justo Gonzalez, *Manana: Christian Theology from a Hispanic Perspective* (Nashville: Abingdon Press, 1990), 113–114.
9. There has been a renaissance of sorts in recent decades in the theological literature focused on understanding God from a Trinitarian perspective. If you are interested in reading more in this area I would highly recommend *God for Us: The Trinity and Christian Life* (San Francisco: HarperSanFrancisco, 1993) by the late theologian Catherine Lacugna. It's a terrific book.

Chapter 2

1. For a sampling of the literature in the field of congregational studies, see Nancy Ammerman, *Congregation & Community* (Rutgers University Press, 1997); Jim Wind and James Lewis, eds., *American Congregations* (University of Chicago Press, 1994); and Nancy Ammerman, Jackson Carroll, Carl Dudley, and William McKinney, eds., *Studying Congregations: A New Handbook* (Nashville: Abingdon Press, 1998).

2. With regard to this undercurrent of individualism, see especially Parker Palmer, *The Company of Strangers* (New York: Crossroad, 1981); Robert N. Bellah et al. *Habits of the Heart* (New York: Harper & Row, 1985); and Robert Putnam, *Bowling Alone: The Collapse and Revival of American Community* (New York: Simon & Schuster, 2000).

3. Edwin Friedman, *Generation to Generation: Family Process in Church and Synagogue* (New York: The Guilford Press, 1985), 195.

4. Wolfhart Pannenberg, *Anthropology in Theological Perspective*, Matthew J. O'Connell, trans. (Philadelphia: Westminster John Knox Press, 1985), 71. See also Luther's explanation to the first commandment in his Large Catechism in Theodore Tappert, ed., *The Book of Concord* (Philadelphia: Fortress Press, 1959), 365.

5. Herbert Anderson, review of Edwin H. Friedman's *Generation to Generation: Family Process in Church and Synagogue* in *Pastoral Psychology* 37 (Fall 1988): 61–62.

6. Paul Hanson, *The People Called: The Growth of Community in the Bible* (Louisville, Ky.: Westminster John Knox Press, 2001).

Chapter 3

1. These comments were made by Stanley Hauer at an Emergent theological conversation in Chapel Hill, N.C., January 20–22, 2003.

2. Martin Buber, *I and Thou*, trans. Walter Kaufman (New York: Touchstone, 1971). This book is a classic and well worth a look some time.

3. This beautiful image, along with a couple of others used in this section, comes from Daniel Erlander, *Baptized We Live: Lutheranism as a Way of Life* (DVD: Daniel Erlander, 1981; 1995).

4. Erlander, *Baptized We Live.*

5. Robert Jenson, *Story and Promise* (Philadelphia: Fortress Press, 1973), 23.

6. Robert Kolb, Timothy Wengert, eds., James Schaaf, ed. and trans., "The Apology to the Augsburg Confession: Article IV, On Justification," in

The Book of Concord: The Confessions of the Evangelical Lutheran Church (Minneapolis: Augsburg Fortress, 2001). This is one of many places in the writings of Luther and the reformers that supports the essential theological point being made here.

7. Flannery O'Connor, *The Habit of Being: Letters of Flannery O'Connor,* Sally Fitzgerald, ed. (New York: The Noonday Press, 1988).

8. Brian McLaren, "Story," *NEXT* Special Edition (Tyler, Tex.: Leadership Network, 1999): 6.

Chapter 4

1. A phrase coined by Brian McLaren, now the title-before-the-colon of one of his recent books.

2. The growth in the emergent network—whose tagline is "a growing generative friendship among missional Christian leaders"—is evidence, at least in part, of this propensity. Join the conversation at www.emergentvillage.com.

3. I'm nervous about these broad, generational categories even as I use them, but some kind of language is needed to begin to describe, at least sociologically, the texture of these communities. The disclaimer is that "generational" language represents a conceptual category, one among many, intended to help with sociological description. It is limited and certainly not definitive.

4. For an interesting take on some of these differences visit http://www. georgetown.edu/faculty/irvinem/technoculture/pomo.html. I'm not trying to be cute here, but rather to suggest that "post" language is often used uncritically when all other language seems to fail.

5. In deconstructionist theory, consult Derrida or Lacan; in politics, Foucault; social theory, Baudrillard; architecture, Jencks; literature, Barthes; philosophy, Rorty or Lyotard. My point is that there are many different perspectives on the various forms of "post" language that is used.

6. This way of seeing evidence of the shifts that have taken place comes from Graeme Codrington, "Living in an Age of Transition" (Online, 2000) http://codrington.biz/lutheracademy/transition.htm.

7. Peter Drucker, *Post-Capitalist Society* (New York: Harper Collins, 1993), 1.

8. Webster says about dogma: An authoritative principle, belief, or statement of ideas or opinion, especially one considered to be absolutely true. Pop culture says about dogma: *Dogma* the movie www.dogma-movie.com or www.imdb.com/title/tt0120655.

9. William M Easum, *The Church of the 21st Century* (Online, 1993) www.easum.com/bybill/Church21.htm, 23 (site now discontinued).

10. Latin for "order." The term is used to refer to an order of service, the classical expression of which in Christian worship is gathering, word, meal, and sending.

11. Follow this link and you will find an interesting article on the relationship between worship and the arts: www.next-wave.org/apr00/musings_on_art.htm.

12. Webster says: discursive \dis-KUR-siv\, adjective: 2. Utilizing, marked by, or based on analytical reasoning—contrasted with intuitive.

13. Webster says: 1: not concerned with religion or religious purposes.

14. *Keeping the Faith*, Touchstone Home Entertainment, 2000.

15. http://en.wikipedia.org/wiki/Lectio_Divina. This link to a Wikipedia article is certainly not definitive, but will serve as a gateway for gathering information and accessing additional web links.

16. For a few samples visit www.apostleschurch.org/about_beliefs.php or http://jacobswellchurch.org/beliefs or http://threads.ccbchurch.com/app/w_page.php?id=3&type=section.

17. Webster says: guiding star; something that serves as a model or guide.

18. Loren Mead, *Five Challenges for the Once and Future Church* (Washington, D.C.: The Alban Institute, 1996).

19. Pete Ward, *Liquid Church* (Peabody, Mass.: Hendrickson Publishers, 2002).

20. Ward, *Liquid Church*, 49.

21. Scholar Robert Webber, as much as anyone today, has explored and reflected on this ancient-future impulse. Visit www.ancientfutureworship.com.

22. The seminal work is: Hans-Georg Gadamer, *Truth and Method*, 2nd rev. ed. (Continuum International Publishing Group, 2005).

Chapter 5

1. The insights in the first part of this paragraph are a brief summary from: William Easum, *Sacred Cows Make Gourmet Burgers* (Nashville: Abingdon Press, 1996), 19–29.

2. Leonard Sweet, "The Movies, T-Rex and Vibrational Leadership," *NetFax*, 17 March (1997): 3.

3. Loren B. Mead, *The Once and Future Church* (Washington, D.C.: The Alban Institute, 1991), 4–5.

4. Carl F. George, *Prepare Your Church for the Future* (Grand Rapids, Mich.: Fleming H. Revell, 1992), 185.

5. For a more thorough survey of the various theories of leadership see Ronald A. Heifetz, *Leadership without Easy Answers* (Cambridge, Mass.: The Belknap Press, 1994), 13–27.

6. Augsburg Confession, Ger. VII:1 in *The Book of Concord,* 32. [Augsburg Confession, Article 7, paragraph 1.] Reference here is to the older Tappert edition.

7. Cheryl Peterson, "Whither Lutheran Ecclesiology?" *Trinity Seminary Review* 27/2 (2006): 107–20. I would encourage you to read the article to see the full scope of her proposal.

8. Peterson, "Whither Lutheran Ecclesiology?" 109.

9. Leonard Sweet, *FaithQuakes* (Nashville: Abingdon Press, 1994), 142.

10. Ibid.

11. Joseph Sittler, *Gravity and Grace* (Minneapolis: Augsburg Publishing House, 1986), 52.

12. *The Matrix Reloaded,* Warner Brothers, 2003.

13. For an excellent, theologically solid treatment of this see Martha Ellen Stortz, *PastorPower* (Nashville: Abingdon Press, 1993).

Additional Resources

Books

Bass, Diane Butler. *Christianity for the Rest of Us: How the Neighborhood Church Is Transforming the Faith* (HarperSanFrancisco, 2006).

———. *The Practicing Congregation: Imagining a New Old Church* (The Alban Institute, 2004).

Bolger, Ryan and Eddie Gibbs. *Emerging Churches: Creating Christian Community in Postmodern Cultures* (Baker Academic, 2005).

Frost, Michael and Alan Hirsch. *The Shaping of Things to Come: Innovation and Mission for the 21st Century Church* (Hendrickson Publishers, 2003).

Hunter, George. *The Celtic Way of Evangelism: How Christianity Can Reach the West . . . Again* (Abingdon Press, 2000).

McLaren, Brian. *A New Kind of Christian; The Story We Find Ourselves In; The Last Word and the Word After That* (Jossey-Bass, 2005). N.B.: This is a boxed set.

Miller, Donald. *Blue Like Jazz: Nonreligious Thoughts on Christian Spirituality* (Nelson Books, 2003).

Sedmak, Clemens. *Doing Local Theology: A Guide for Artisans of a New Humanity* (Orbis Books, 2002).

Ward, Pete. *Liquid Church* (Hendrickson Publishers, 2002).

Periodicals and e-zines

"Emergent Church: A Visit to Jacob's Well." *The Christian Century*, Vol. 123, No. 19 (September 19, 2006): 20–24.

Next-Wave~Church & Culture, www.the-next-wave-ezine.info.

"What is the Emergent Church." *The Christian Century*, Vol. 121, No. 24 (November 30, 2004): 20–31.

Websites of some emerging church communities

Church of the Apostles, www.apostleschurch.org.

ekklesia, www.ecclesiahouston.org.

Jacobs Well, http://jacobswellchurch.org.

Solomons Porch, www.solomonsporch.com.

Weblogs

A blog is a user-generated Web site where entries are made in journal style and displayed in a reverse chronological order. Here are a couple of links to some prolific, provocative bloggers.

Johnny Baker, http://jonnybaker.blogs.com.

Tallskinnykiwi (Andrew Jones), http://tallskinnykiwi.typepad.com.

Karen Ward, www.submergence.org.

Tony Jones, http://theoblogy.blogspot.com.

Virtual Communities (Networks)

Emergent Village, www.emergentvillage.com, is a growing, generative friendship among missional Christian leaders seeking to love our world in the spirit of Jesus Christ.

Emerging Leaders Network, www.emergingleadersnetwork.org, is a community of friendship, exploration, and theological conversation among people interested in emerging churches and faith communities.

The Ooze, www.theooze.com, is conversation for the journey.

Need more information about any terms or language used here? Try www.wikipedia.org.

Other books in the Lutheran Voices series

Other books (continued)

978-0-8066-4990-0	Susan K. Hedahl *Who Do You Say That I Am? 21st Century Preaching*
978-0-8066-4997-9	Mary E. Hinkle *Signs of Belonging: Luther's Marks of the Church and the Christian Life*
978-0-8066-5172-9	Robert F. Holley & Paul E. Walters *Called by God to Serve: Reflections for Church Leaders*
978-0-8066-8001-9	Timothy F. Lull *On Being Lutheran: Reflections on Church, Theology, and Faith*
978-0-8066-8003-3	Nancy Maeker & Peter Rogness *Ending Poverty: A 20/20 Vision*
978-0-8066-4994-8	Martin E. Marty *Speaking of Trust: Conversing with Luther about the Sermon on the Mount*
978-0-8066-4999-3	Rochelle Melander & Harold Eppley *Our Lives Are Not Our Own: Saying "Yes" to God*
978-0-8066-4987-0	Cynthia Moe-Lobeda *Public Church: For the Life of the World*
978-0-8066-5333-4	Carolyn Coon Mowchan *Holy Purpose: The Blessings of Service, Obedience, and Faith*
978-0-8066-4996-2	Carolyn Coon Mowchan & Damian Anthony Vraniak *Connecting with God in a Disconnected World: A Guide for Spiritual Growth and Renewal*
978-0-8066-4993-1	Craig L. Nessan *Give Us This Day: A Lutheran Proposal for Ending World Hunger*
978-0-8066-4934-4	Alvin Rogness *Living in the Kingdom: Reflections on Luther's Catechism*
978-0-8066-5111-8	William Russell *Praying for Reform: Luther, Prayer, and the Christian Life*
978-0-8066-5173-6	Joseph Sittler *Gravity and Grace: Reflections and Provocations*
978-0-8066-8002-6	Paul A. Wee *American Destiny and the Calling of the Church*

See www.lutheranvoices.com